Katūīvei
Contemporary Pasifika Poetry from Aotearoa New Zealand

Edited by David Eggleton,
Vaughan Rapatahana and Mere Taito

MASSEY UNIVERSITY PRESS

Contents

Nau mai haere mai
ngā manuhiri mai i ngā takutai katoa.
Mātaki i ngā kupu,
whakaaroaro i ngā tirohanga,
whakamiha i ngā tāwara,
ako i ngā oro
o Te Moananui-a-Kiwa mārohirohi.
Tomo mai tētahi me te katoa
i roto i te whakamīharo
o *Katūīvei*.

Welcome welcome
visitors from all shores.
Consider the words,
contemplate the sights,
appreciate the flavours,
study the sounds
of the mighty Pacific Ocean.
Enter one and all
into the wonderment
of *Katūīvei*.

Introduction

Aotearoa New Zealand is home to many peoples of the Pasifika diaspora. We began gradually arriving in numbers from the Moana Nui — from the Cook Islands, Niue, Tokelau, Sāmoa, Tonga, Vanuatu and other archipelagos — as migrants after the Second World War, seeking a shot at the Western dream in return for our cheap labour. Now, there are first-, second-, third- and even fourth-generation descendants living here, in what the poet Courtney Sina Meredith has called 'Urbanesia'. Pasifika peoples represent almost 10 per cent of the population, are one of the fastest growing demographic groups in the country, and contribute profoundly to New Zealand society in all kinds of ways, including through a vibrant efflorescence of cultural activity, from music and dance to art, theatre, film and literature.

And within that literature, like a vital thread, runs poetry. *Katūīvei: Contemporary Pasifika Poetry from Aotearoa New Zealand* is a celebration of one of the most exciting developments in recent New Zealand poetry. In bringing together this fresh compilation drawn from the past decade, our kaupapa has been to highlight something of the diversity and complexity of Pasifika heritage evidenced by poetic voices who write in the English language: from the South Auckland Poetry Collective to Polynation and slam poetry; from the individual successes and mana of John Puhiatau Pule, Selina Tusitala Marsh, Tusiata Avia, Karlo Mila, Courtney Sina Meredith, Serie Barford and David Eggleton to the burgeoning reputations of poets such as Grace Iwashita-Taylor, Rita Masae, Daren Kamali, Rob Hack and Mere Taito; and from the poems of former rough sleepers to the challenging poems of younger writers.

We follow in the wake of a succession of path-finding anthologies, and any anthology of modern Pasifika literature must acknowledge the central importance and early inspirational example of Albert Wendt, who has been committed to establishing the importance of Oceanic-Pacific writing. Beginning with *Lali: A Pacific Anthology* in 1980, he has nurtured the vā, the interconnections between language and place, literature and belonging. He also edited *Nuanua: Pacific Writing in English Since 1980*, published in 1995, and then co-edited, again with Rena Whaitiri and Robert Sullivan, *Whetu Moana: Contemporary Polynesian Poems in English*, which was published in 2003. In 2010, also with Reina Whaitiri and Robert Sullivan, he co-edited *Mauri Ola: Contemporary Polynesian Poems in English*. Albert Wendt remains a leading poet and writer of Oceania, of the Moana Nui and, by extension, of world literature.

The title of our anthology, *Katūīvei*, is a hybrid term, a combination of the Rotuman word 'kavei' and the pan-Pacific word 'tūī'. Kavei means to steer by or wayfind: to navigate. Tūī is the bird of Aotearoa that has a dual voice box and hence two voices, symbolic of the complexities Pasifika poets and peoples must negotiate every day. To write poetry in Niu Sila as a Pacific migrant is an act of wayfinding, a creative process of discovery and negotiation between cultural spaces.

This may be the first anthology of contemporary Oceanic-Pacific poets who live in Aotearoa New Zealand but it is not that these poets have all just leapt from an ocean-going, double-hulled vaka grounded on a beach in these islands. However, they do share genealogies, communal traditions and experiences and family memories and stories that are specifically Pasifika within a multicultural society that shapes their outlook. These are poets of the Pasifika diaspora who have settled here, or who were born and raised here, or who have lived here for substantial amounts of time, while toing and froing elsewhere. They are poets with modern lives who sometimes have a complicated relationship with their Pasifika heritage.

We wanted this anthology to be inclusive, to provide room for as many Pasifika poetic voices as possible. And we wanted to create a balanced anthology representative of many viewpoints and many styles, showing Pasifika poetry to be in a constant state of 'old and new', of haharągi and lelea' mafua, a lively and evolving continuum.

Because Māori are tangata whenua, the people of the land, they are not included as part of this recent Pasifika migration narrative. Māori literature has its own historical continuum in this land that goes back into the mists of time and forward into the future. ('Kia whakatōmuri te haere whakamua': 'I walk backwards into the future with my eyes fixed on my past'.) Pasifika peoples are new arrivals, tauiwi or manuhiri (guests who share in the bounty of the land), with separate but related cultural practices. However, Māori poets who have Pasifika migrant heritage have been included, of course.

Katūīvei, which is intended to be a record of what is happening now or in the immediate past, capturing poems on the wing, came about through talanoa or conversations between us, and other poets and writers were also consulted and expressed their views. As editors we bring similar as well as diverse points of view, although every anthology is inevitably a product of its time and circumstances and historical context. Many community-led and small-press publications played an advocacy role in bringing Pasifika poets to our attention.

We wanted to present a sense of excitement and transformation and confidence about the present moment: for example, it is both appropriate and serendipitous that the first poem in this book, by Marina Alefosio, was written for and performed at the official ceremony for the New Zealand government apology for the infamous dawn raids of the mid-1970s, held at Auckland Town Hall on 1 August 2021.

We have worked on this anthology for a number of years, endeavouring to locate all poetry by Pasifika poets in this country that has appeared since 2012, with more emphasis on very recent work up to the end of 2022. David Eggleton is a former Aotearoa New Zealand Poet Laureate of Pasifika heritage who spent some of his formative years growing up in Fiji. His maternal grandmother was from Maʻufanga on the island of Tongatapu, and his maternal grandfather was from Mofmairo on the island of Rotuma. Vaughan Rapatahana (Te Āti Awa, Ngāti Te Whiti), who has been involved with editing various anthologies, including a 2023 compilation of Māori writing and a recent anthology of Cook Islander poetry, brings this experience to bear, as well as his understanding as tangata whenua. Mere Taito (Rotuma: Malha'a ma Noa'tau) brings her Pasifika perspective as an interdisciplinary creative practice scholar and poet based in Kirikiriroa Hamilton. She is originally from the island of Rotuma in Fiji and has lived in New Zealand for the past fourteen years.

Naturally, these backgrounds, interests and approaches produced an enormous number of possible poems, which we had to make manageable. We chose more poems from established poets, but with an upper limit of three, and sometimes choices were difficult. Because of the diversity of narratives and themes, which were often echoed, interconnected or intertwined with other mahi in complex and nuanced ways, the poems appear in the alphabetical order of their poets' surnames.

Some poets published here — Gina Cole and Victor Rodger, for example — are better known in other genres, but they have also produced strong, inspirational poems in recent times. Among our poets, too, are a number of Pasifika tamaiti — school students — including Kalisolaite Fonongaloa and Sakaraia Nasau, and we confidently expect the numbers of young Pasifika poets to grow in the future, emerging from the generally supportive Pacific studies and creative writing educational environments in this country.

We read and researched with the joy of discovery as we encountered some extraordinary talent. Wananavu! We worked both together and independently as editors in order to arrive at a consensus for each and every poem included here, sometimes after much debate and reconsideration. Above all, as an editorial panel, we sought to provide a sense of the oceanic sweep of accomplishment of Pasifika poetry in this country now, in all its liveliness and variety.

Vinaka vakalevu. Malo 'aupito. Fạiȧkse'ea ma ạlạlum. Ngā mihi nui.

David Eggleton
Vaughan Rapatahana
Mere Taito

A brief history of Pasifika poetry in Aotearoa

The first Pasifika poet of the modern diaspora to emerge in Aotearoa New Zealand was Alistair Te Ariki Campbell, who was born in Rarotonga in 1925 and who died in Wellington in 2009. His father was a trader from Dunedin and of Scottish ancestry. His mother was from Tongareva in the northern group of the Cook Islands.

Campbell came to New Zealand at the age of eight with his siblings, after the death of both of his parents. The children grew up in an orphanage in Dunedin. Campbell began writing poetry at high school, and in 1950, after graduating from university, he became the first Polynesian poet to have a collection of his poems published in English. This book, *Mine Eyes Dazzle*, published by Pegasus Press, was critically acclaimed and led to Campbell being acknowledged as 'a master of language'.

For those of the Pasifika diaspora, there is the Pacific we carry in our heads and there is a Pacific which is the site of various contestations. Campbell encountered racism in his daily life in mid-twentieth-century New Zealand, and subsequently downplayed his Polynesian identity, but his early poems are lyrical and rhythmic and animistic in a way that draws directly on his Polynesian background and intuitions. One of his best-known early poems, 'The Return', is full of foreboding as it speaks of 'the surf-loud beach', 'mats and splintered masts', 'plant gods, tree gods', and 'fires going out on the thundering sand'.

Campbell's sense of alienation from his Polynesian roots — 'the Polynesian strain' as he called it — contributed to a series of nervous breakdowns that took him years to overcome, and the healing process as a creative writer involved his return to Rarotonga for the first time in 1976. This led to a new creative efflorescence, beginning with his collection *Dark Lord of Savaiki*, published by Te Kotare Press in 1980.

The Cook Islands, Niue and Tokelau have a special relationship with New Zealand, established in the colonial era. As a result, their citizens are New Zealand citizens and have the legal right to live here. Those from Sāmoa, Tonga and elsewhere in the Pacific require visas. The mid-1970s are now remembered as the era of 'dawn raids', when heavy-handed immigration officials targeted Pacific Islanders in their homes in the early morning in search of those whose visas had expired.

But by the mid-1970s New Zealand had also become a country with a sizeable Polynesian population, and a new cultural assertiveness had begun to manifest itself. Pacific Island groups, such as the Polynesian Panther Party and members of various church denominations, established themselves as community activists, aligning with other political activists such as the Nuclear-Free Pacific movement and the anti-Springbok Tour movement, as well as with protesters seeking Māori self-determination and recognition of land rights. Colonial legacies began to be questioned and challenged.

In 1976 Albert Wendt, recently appointed lecturer at the newly-established University of the South Pacific in Fiji, produced his landmark declaration 'Towards a New Oceania', which called for the recognition of an Indigenous Polynesian literature. It was printed in the inaugural issue of *Mana Review: A South Pacific Journal of Language and Literature*, produced by the University of the South Pacific Press. In this manifesto Wendt stated: 'Our quest should not be for a revival of our past cultures but for the creation of new cultures which are free of the taint of colonialism and based firmly on our own pasts. The quest should be for a new Oceania.'

Wendt was born in Apia, Sāmoa, and moved to New Plymouth, New Zealand, as a scholarship student in 1953, when he was thirteen years old. The publication of his acclaimed first novel, *Sons for the Return Home*, in 1973 was a defining event for modern Pasifika literature, establishing Wendt as a pre-eminent Polynesian writer. In 1976, the publishing firm Longman Paul in Auckland released Albert Wendt's first poetry collection, *Inside Us the Dead: Poems 1961 to 1974*. Like Alistair Campbell, Wendt had begun writing poems at high school.

In 1980 a weekly poetry reading event called Poetry Live, open to all, was established by the Pālagi poet David Mitchell at the since demolished Globe Hotel in inner-city Auckland. This lively and popular performance space featuring established poets as guest readers soon attracted a variety of younger Pasifika poets to read their work, including David Eggleton, John Pule, Albert Livingston Refiti, Serie Barford and Gina Cole. David Eggleton was already producing self-published broadsheets of his poems, while John Pule produced his first self-published poetry pamphlet, *Sonnets to Van Gogh*, in 1982.

Eggleton and Pule began occasionally performing together, busking their poems at venues such as Cook Street Market. In 1983 they launched a national poetry performance tour as *Two South Auckland Polynesian Poets* (Eggleton grew up partly in Māngere East, while Pule grew up partly in Ōtara), supported by what was then the Māori and South Pacific Arts Council. Later that year, both poets took part in a key series of readings by Indigenous writers entitled 'Māori Writers Read' at the Depot Theatre in Wellington, alongside Alistair Te Ariki Campbell, Witi Ihimaera, Apirana Taylor, Patricia Grace and others.

Like Campbell and Wendt, as Pasifika poets and storytellers Eggleton and Pule were products of the colonial classroom, having its stereotyping and profiling drummed into them and consequently struggling to deal with a sense of cultural diminishment and imbalance. As Albert Wendt stated in the *Mana Review* manifesto, it was necessary 'to free ourselves of the mythologies created about us in colonial literature'.

Other Pasifika writers, too, felt the pressure. In an interview with Maryanne Pale on Creative Talanoa, Serie Barford described how she struggled to cope with the New Zealand university system: 'I was brought up the old way with the church and with chaperones and found myself alone in a strange place at the height of the feminist movement in the late 1970s. Every time I opened my mouth in a tutorial I felt like I was being mocked and that my world view was being ridiculed.'

Gradually, though, things began to change, especially after the 1984 election of the progressive Fourth Labour Government under David Lange and the subsequent declaration of a nuclear-free New Zealand, which helped establish a new sense of identity based in the South Pacific. However, overcoming conservative prejudices remained a work in progress; Pacific Islanders continued to be treated as political scapegoats in the media and continued to be confronted by urban alienation, economic disadvantages and a precarious migrant status. For the dominant Pākehā settler culture, the Pacific persisted as an exotic 'elsewhere' and Britain remained 'the mother country'.

But by the early 1990s, evidence of the cultural turn towards Aotearoa New Zealand's geographical location as a South Pacific nation was being acknowledged more and more. David Eggleton's first collection of poems, *South Pacific Sunrise*, was published by Penguin Books in 1986; it was co-winner of the Jessie Mackay Best First Book Award for Poetry the following year. Albert Wendt returned to New Zealand as Professor of New Zealand Literature at the University of Auckland in 1988. Samoan poet and artist Momoe Malietoa Von Reiche, then living in Northland, became notable in 1989 when New Women's Press published a substantial collection of her poetry, *Tai — Heart of a Tree*. John Pule's first novel, *The Shark that Ate the Sun (Ko E Mago Ne Kai E La)*, was published by Penguin in 1992.

Pacific Islanders were now becoming prominent in many cultural areas of endeavour in Niu Sila, from dance and theatre to art and music. The rock band Herbs, founded in 1979 by Samoan vocalist and songwriter Toni Fonoti — who said he wanted 'to put Pacific influences into music, make Island culture more available, give it a modern soul' — produced a number of anthemic recordings, including the era-defining, anti-nuclear-testing protest song 'French Letter'.

In the 1990s there was a surge of Pasifika musical artists creating highly articulate rap lyrics and song lyrics commenting on social issues — from Sisters Underground (with Brenda Pua) and OMC (Pauly Fuemana) to King Kapisi, Che Fu and the group Nesian Mystik. In

Papatoetoe, South Auckland, the recording label Dawn Raid Entertain-
ment, repurposing traumatic memories of the dawn raids, signed up a
raft of Pasifika hip-hop artists and released their party and dance music.

Community-activist Pasifika poets of the 1990s included Reverend
Mua Strickson-Pua, an ordained church minister who mentored Pasifika
youth at the Tagata Pasifika Resource Centre in Auckland, encouraging
them as poets and performers. Rosanna Raymond was another artist,
writer and poet who came to prominence in the mid-1990s in Auckland
as a founding member of the Pacific Sisters art collective, celebrating
mana wāhine.

In 2000, Teresia Kieuea Teaiwa was appointed the inaugural
programme director of Pacific Studies at Victoria University in
Wellington. A poet, theorist and academic, Teaiwa grew up as part of the
resettled Banaban community on the island of Rabi in Fiji and undertook
postgraduate university studies in the United States. Like Albert Wendt
earlier, in the 1990s she became a pivotal figure in connecting Pasifika
literatures across Oceania as a regular presenter at conferences and
other events, using the concept of the vā.

In his 1993 essay 'Our Sea of Islands', published in the book
A New Oceania: Rediscovering Our Sea of Islands produced by the
University of the South Pacific Press, Tongan writer Epeli Hauʻofa,
a leading light based in Suva, pointed out that nineteenth-century
imperialism erected boundaries that led to the contraction of Oceania,
'transforming a once boundless world into states and territories'. A
return to Indigenous concepts was needed to re-establish a sense of
unity and interconnectedness, he wrote. The vā is just such a concept;
it's the traditional dynamic space that holds Pasifika peoples together as
a group; it is the sea between islands.

In his 1993 novel *Ola*, Albert Wendt wrote about the vā as a
metaphor for connection, integral to Polynesian thought, serving to
define relationships:

> Our vā with others define us.
> We can only be ourselves linked to everyone and everything
> else in the Vā, the-Unity-that-is-All and now.

Wendt proposed the vā as acknowledging a vast interconnecting faka-papa, recognising the interrelational spaces between people and their environment as an act of imagination. As he wrote in 1976 in *Towards a New Oceania*: 'Oceania deserves more than an attempt at mundane fact; only the imagination in free flight can hope — if not to contain her — to grasp some of her shape, plumage, and pain.'

Teaiwa echoed this sentiment, stating in an 2015 interview with the journalist Dale Husband for *E-Tangata*: 'It's my job to remind people of the complexity [of the Pacific] and not let them try to paint us with a single brush stroke.' The Moana Nui is a complex hybrid entity, and we have sought to represent this paradoxical reality through the editorial mix of contemporary poems in *Katūīvei*.

In 2001, poet Doug Poole produced the first issue of *Blackmail Press* as an online poetry journal, with special emphasis on Polynesian creative writing. Even with its slightly erratic publishing schedule, *Blackmail Press* today remains an important internet platform for showcasing new talent, an integral part of the Pasifika digital vā.

In 2002, Tusiata Avia, recently returned from a decade travelling overseas, created the first iteration of her solo poetry show *Wild Dogs Under My Skirt*, and in 2004 her debut collection of poems under the same title was published by Victoria University Press. Over the next few years, *Wild Dogs Under My Skirt* was presented by Avia at arts festivals around the world. In 2019, a multiple-actor version of *Wild Dogs Under My Skirt*, produced by Victor Rodger, won The Fringe Encore Series Outstanding Production of the Year at the Soho Playhouse in New York; once marginalised, Pasifika poetry had stepped onto global centre stage.

In 2003, when *Whetu Moana: Contemporary Polynesian Poems in English*, edited by Albert Wendt, Reina Whaitiri and Robert Sullivan, appeared, it was described as 'the first anthology of contemporary Indigenous Polynesian poetry in English edited by Polynesians'. It catalogued and celebrated poets whose work had been published over the previous twenty years, revealing common themes and concerns around dispossession, displacement, marginality, adaption, negotiation — and the process of reclaiming the Indigenous voice.

In 2006, Karlo Mila's first collection of poems, *Dream Fish Floating*, won the Jessie Mackay Best First Book Award for Poetry at the Montana New Zealand Book Awards. This collection mapped the psychogeography of Oceania as a work in progress, and being 'Tongan' as a state of mind as well as a 'bloodline thing'. Mila was one of the nine poets in the Pasifika Poets Collective who took part in the 2008 Polynation show, created by Doug Poole and directed by Tusiata Avia, and she presented first at the Queensland Poetry Festival in Brisbane and then at the Going West Festival in Auckland. Other poets performing with Polynation included the Reverend Mua Strickson-Pua, Serie Barford, Daren Kamali and Selina Tusitala Marsh, who performed her now-canonical poem 'Fast-Talking PI'.

Fast-Talking PI became the title of Marsh's debut collection of poems, which won the Jessie Mackay Best First Book Award for Poetry in 2009. Over the past decade, Marsh, who was New Zealand's first Pasifika Poet Laureate (2017–19), has become known for her energetic and inspiring poetry performances, as well establishing herself as an influential figure through her teaching of Pasifika literature at Waipapa Taumata Rau University of Auckland, where, succeeding Albert Wendt, she is a professor in the English and Drama Department.

In 2008, the South Auckland Poets Collective was founded by Grace Iwashita-Taylor and Daren Kamali, with Ramon Narayan, as part of a Youthline initiative, and it remains active today with around fourteen members and a large Pasifika component. Other Pasifika writing groups have since sprung up in many communities, towns and suburbs.

By the beginning of the second decade of the millennium, Pasifika poetry had undeniably become a major presence in New Zealand literature, helping to illuminate our understanding of Aotearoa New Zealand and its place in the world on a number of levels and in a variety of ways. Spoken-word events, poetry slam nights and performance poetry presentations have all been enlivened by Pasifika writers, while local Pasifika poets such as Leilani Tamu, Courtney Sina Meredith, Simone Kaho, Grace Iwashita-Taylor, Daren Kamali and Faumuina

Felolini Maria Tafuna'i have all brought out significant and substantial debut collections of poems over the past decade to present the variety of moods, atmospheres and concerns of Pasifika life in Niu Sila Aotearoa New Zealand today.

David Eggleton

Poems

Marina Alefosio

Raiding the Dawn

Who is worthy of the first light?
The break of day?
A new beginning?
If our value is measured by the pigment of our skin or the origin of our
story — who gets to decide how that story is analysed? Captured in text?
Bound in history books? And resold to generations and generations?
Citizenship is a process, but people are not products.
Our value is not in the factory hand gripping the pen, signing the
immigration paper, breaking the border or picking up the new language.
We broke borders with broken accents to break the chains of fear, a fear
of the future.
We worked and we work in these factories, these systems with values
seamed into our pockets, written in the tablets of our hearts with joy
because we had the future in our foresight.
We signed the papers with the faith of tomorrow.
And we woke up
And we wake up every day with the promise of that first light for our
children, our grandchildren, the children of our neighbours, of our
hosts, our brothers and sisters — tangata whenua.
The livelihood of a nation is found in our waking.
So when the dark moved in and the light moved out and we were faced
with another separation, we became like soil — marred by the dirt
written and campaigned about us — stigmatised for daring to dream —
daring to voyage — daring to wake up next to our loved ones.
Again citizenship is a process, but families are not products.
So when our dawn was raided and the blue hues and the red hues came
in and that palette in the sky was shaken by the sounds of cracked eyes,
heart palpitations, a brother hidden there, a pregnant woman waiting in
the cells over there with no milk to feed her child, a cousin looking for
coins to call his family to tell them he was found out and waiting at the
departure gate, ready to go back while his Papa hid in the room praying.

We went back to those values seamed into our pockets, pulled out our
roots and remembered who were were
And we went back to work, we went back to serve, to do the thing that we
came here to do
And if you ever measured our value by our service, you would be amazed
at the stars you cannot count like the nations Abraham in the Old
Testament could not account for with his human eyes or his servant heart
Who is worthy of a quality life?
Who gets to determine what that looks like?
Let it be known that healing is a process and forgiveness is not a product
— it's a promise.
We are looking for a true Genesis
Standing at the arrival gates,
Taking back our dawn
Handing it down to our descendants
Along with our values
Our servanthood leadership
Warm housing
A higher education
Life abundant
Village on the hills
Valleys no longer drying us up
Of our Moana
Te Moana-nui-a-Kiwa
We are all worthy of that first light
We are all worthy of that first light
We are all worthy of that first light!

The Local Theatre

It is true
they CAN make fire with their hands
rubber boys and black tight bandits
fast paced lip service
birthed from leaky homes
holding the heads of their elders
they chant,
ONE OUT, ONE OUT
their adolescent tongues become ropes
tied up in the sizing up of
their own necks
STEP, brother, STEP
stomp, footloose,
free musicals followed by
free media press
I start to foresee it,
one affidavit stapled
to the other
just another day when the word gets around
and when word gets to platform 2
they rush up like crazy 88
with tin can weaponry
this time
my son and I are watching stage left
I feel his forehead
and his temper has heightened too
so much I have to forewarn him
that these boys have mothers too
they're on stage somewhere too,
fighting just as much
to push the blood back down their children,

praying
that this synthetic sight is temporary
I promise him
that bandanas become bibs
any minute now
and it's his time to live
and I honestly cry for years
because I know I can't put it off
just listen out until the day
and continue watching Manurewa erupt
a boil up of almost men

Aziembry Aolani

Parking Warden

My colleague says my skin colour shows that I like rugby.
I tell him, 'I don't follow rugby . . .'
He says, 'Your skin tells *me* though . . .'
My skin has never spoken to anyone.

A man yells from a moving vehicle,
'Get a fucking real job!'
He extends one of his fingers towards me.
That. Is. Talent.

A woman says the job I do is ridiculous.
Despite paying for the wrong space,
she continues to question my presence.
'Like why do you even?'
Is that even a question?
'I'm actually quite odd,' I reply —
awkward and triumphant silence.

I am called a fat shit.
The driver isn't in the best shape himself.
'Why don't you go for a run, ya fat shit!'
He snatches the fresh white print.
I try to catch laughter in the middle of my throat.
I walk almost 30 kilometres a day,
and I'm Polynesian.

At a pedestrian crossing,
I overhear a woman tell her child,
'You see, son. If you work hard at school, you won't have to do a job like that.'
She points to me.
I turn to the child, 'And I have a walkie-talkie!'

The child smiles.
To his mother's evil eye,
I pull a thumbs up.

Two elderly ladies ask for directions.
One lady says, 'Darling, you don't speak the way you look . . .'
The other: 'You're a very polite young man . . . Good for you . . .'
I pity them.

I see taxis on broken yellow lines
double-parked on a one-way street.
A driver spots me and alerts his companions.
'Go, go! The brown one is here!
The brown one is there!'
I see panic spilling out of their ears and exhaust pipes.

'Does anyone give you shit, bro?'
asks a man gripping a can of beer.
'Why would they? Look at you . . .'
I attach a printed headache to a vehicle.
'You're a big dark-skinned brother. No one will give you shit, my kill!'
I have a sudden vision of myself, as fresh kill, on the roof of a parked vehicle.
A mechanic spots me checking resident and coupon zones.
He screams,
'Warden! Warden!'

Just another white jaw rattling to remind me of what I am.

Name
Inspired by lyrics from Meg Mac

Give me my name back,
capitalized,
as a period,
between my half ethnicities.
Give me my name back,
as a beat to my mother's hula,
chiselled into father's taiaha,
just before their vows misplaced.
Give me my name back,
stuck on the end of rolled cigarettes,
filling lungs of coloured young,
flicking ash upon grounds of their dead.
Give me my name back.
The one covered in age:
Family album —
I've forgotten the value of this face.
Give me my name back,
for my supposed ancestry:
Hunters, sailors, navigators,
their movements are denied in me.
Give me my name back,
in my childhood room,
covering the plastered holes,
where these calluses grew.
Give me my name back,
decapitated,
on the rear of father's utility.
It has hosted rust since 1993.
Give me my name back,
I can't go home without it.

Tusiata Avia

Ova-sta-ya

The Tongan rugby player found them hiding in a fridge
he went round to a house in Balmoral yesterday after a tip-off.
One of a team of Tongan rugby players found them in a fridge
after seeing cabbages strewn across the kitchen floor.

Immigration and police were hiding in a fridge
there was a trail of cabbages strewn across the kitchen floor.
We went there and had a look around,
immigration official Kathryn O'Sullivan said

We put a mattress underneath the house
we were trying to avoid detection.
The Tongan rugby player found them hiding in a fridge
there were cabbages strewn across the kitchen floor.

The Tongan rugby team is considering whether to prosecute
the people who harboured them.
The Tongan rugby player urged the remaining immigration officials
and police officers to hand themselves in or face a similar fate.

Three others had previously been found, he said
We're four down and ten to go.

We are the diasporas

No nations, just a mash-up
of all the countries starting with B
Bermuda, Barbados, Belize, Bahamas

everyone is from there
and all the countries starting with T
Trinidad and Tobago, Turkestan, Tonga.

What collection of molecules are you?
Nobody lives there.
You get a prize if you live in the country you are from

from I'm from From
that's my country
I was born in all the countries starting with F

my parents are each a UN genealogy
they met in all the countries starting with E
Ethiopia, Egypt, Eden, the garden of.

I was brought up in all the countries starting with
B, S, V
and now I live in Toronto.

I speak in Arabic and French and Italian
but if you are from Arabia or France or Italy
you may not understand me

my Creole is thicker than yam-jam
peppersoupgumbomambojambo
Italian spoken with an Eritrean accent

underneath it the seething soup of Tigrinya.
You get a prize if you are loving in the country you were born
or the country you grew up in

or the country your parents are from
or the country you would represent at the Olympics
if you were going to the Olympics.

It's true that poetry was once an Olympic event
a bit like Miss Universe where the poets read in ethnic costumes
or bathing suits.

There is a prize for being the most beautiful poet in the world
and that goes to the man from Trinidad and Tobago.
I can't even speak to him

his skin is too shiny, his teeth too white
his eyelashes too curled, his hands too intelligent.
You get a prize if you can speak.

Poly kidz r coming

Boom Shakalaka Shirley Boys are dressed in pink
sharp teeth round their necks

> *Shirley-is-a-girl's-name!*
> *Where's your boyfriend?*

Their taupou is a boy with muscles
chanting:

> *Shirley Boys is coming!*
> *Where's your boyfriend?*

< >

Marlborough Boys are flying Tongans
bicking all da crapes
Marlborough Girls are britty kirls
bicking all da crapes
All da islands to da vineyards
bicking all da crapes
Tonga, Sāmoa, Tokelau
bicking all da crapes
Tuvalu, Niue, PNG
bicking all the crapes

< >

Suga, you wanna fofō? You gonna lie on my table an write da boem?
Apout me? I gotta send money to my fricken family in Sāmoa. Don
worry, no Carona here, I put da cover for your mouf.

See dat taupou? She frow da gaifi up da air and no one catch! Da boy behind her not even look, just too busy look around all da kirls. Might be cut da head off. He's from my family. What a stupid!

< >

The Tongan boys salute and march and cut us with their spears
Tongan mama gets up on stage
red feathers behind her ear
Marlborough vintage on her feet
Mama takes the spear

Cheehooooooooo!

We scream

Cheehooooooooo!

They will rule us like an army

Watch out Marlborough, Tongan Boys are coming
Where's your girlfriend?

< >

Christchurch Samoan girls go

tik tok
tik tok

Throw themselves down on the floor

tik tok
tik tok

The spirits of aiuli enter

tik tok

tik tok

We scream and laugh
and eat chop suey

Cheehoooooooooo!

< >

Bro says, Don't kiss and hug, pretend like you're The Rock, just raise your eyebrow. Remember Corona and measles and the 1918 influenza.

The Villa Girls dance 1918 and die like flies on stage.

I wanna be head girl next year, Mum
all eyes on me
I wanna be the taupou, Mum
Dancing in the middle
Centre. Of. Attention.

< >

We're looking at the white people when they walk past us and it's just different today, ay? We're in the red zone, but it's like the Brown Zone in Christchurch today, ay?

Yeah, uce, we *are* the Brown Zone.

Cheehoooooooooo!

Poly kidz are coming
Where's your vineyard?
Poly kidz are coming
Where's your white zone?

Serie Barford

Hearts and sensitive grass

our hearts are carefully accommodated
the left lung being smaller than the right
so our passions and woes can harbour
our blood beat thrrr-thrump thrr-thrump

but shifting the universe of our mind
a paltry three handspans to our heart
seems a journey too distant for most

even on this blatantly colonised island
where migrants have traversed oceans
and sensitive grass flourishes with passion fruit

when my mother was a school girl
she spoke her mother tongue in class
was sent outside into the blazing sun
to weed sensitive grass as punishment

the thorns ripped her tender flesh
bestowed nettle rash and shame
droplets of blood destined for her heart
nourished the parched field instead

oh she learnt her lesson well
for when I was small she said
the way forward's English
that's your father's lingo
we live in Niu Sila
don't speak my lingo
I don't want you to be hurt

but when I was older
and she was stronger
she changed her mind
drove me for miles after school
to language and culture classes

but by then my tongue had set
into a concrete kiwi accent

everyone laughed when I spoke her lingo
until the world I was tentatively building
collapsed under layers of well-aimed scorn

now I crouch under the blazing sun
prod sensitive grass with sticks and fingers
blow on it like gentle and harsh winds

estimate how much force it takes for a frond
to fold in response to the outside world

create strategies for dealing with thorns

calculate the distance I'll need to travel
in order to retrieve and free my stifled tongue!

Say my name without the 'sh'

mum ignored advice not to pick me up when I cried
because it won't make her a strong girl in a harsh world

I know this because I've found photos of mum
cradling me when I'm distressed

she read Dr Spock's book on childcare

stumbling over unfamiliar English phrases
that held the key to successful childrearing

on an island where people had names like Tom, Dick, Harry
Hone, Janet, Margery, Glenda, Betty, Pita, Tui and Trev
and ate Sunday roasts cooked by women trussed in aprons

I don't understand why my parents christened me 'Cherie'
when my Samoan grandmother couldn't make the 'sh' sound

when grandma died I changed my name to 'Serie'

when people address me I hear her
laughing and calling across the ocean
Serie!   Serie!   Serie!

Into the world of light

I resolutely lanced my heart
a swollen fist about to burst

with a shark tooth plucked from a dream

poured honey into the first chamber

soothed gnawed memories
sent them west with wild bees

insulated the second chamber with foliage

kawakawa hearts blanketed loss
tempered feelings of abandonment

painted the third chamber gold

ground turmeric mixed with coconut oil
loosened inflammation's angry grip

poulticed the fourth chamber with suka

toxins drawn into a sweet citadel
dissolved into spontaneous sun showers

bandaged myself with banana leaves
waded into the ocean

the shark tooth pulsed
warned off predators

suspended beyond the measure of clocks

floating

floating

floating

until my grandmother's kingfisher brough me ashore

embraced by pouliuli

my ruptured casement of grief
flew into the world of light

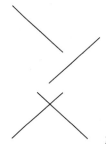
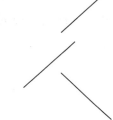

Pelenakeke Brown
Crossings

My maternal grandmother died the same day I was born.

I carry her name in my blood // breath
When you invoke me, you are also calling to her.
I miss breathing life into my other nanas name too,
I hope my future pepe might carry a memory of her name.

totõ: implant/set   toto: blood

with the passing of blood,
with the birth of life,
you are implanting a new seed
with
manavā

My mother says my grandmother died
from losing too much blood
My birth record says I was distressed

My mother won't speak much about this time

I told them the baby was coming, but they said no.
I told them the baby was coming, but they said no.

I believe something happened in that channel
of manavā   and māsū
the breath   with the slowing down
of new life   hardened, dying breath of another.

during this passage of time,   and travel, between the worlds
pulotu   and   lalolagi
there was a crossing

a splitting

Taema and Tilafaigā experienced a splitting
when they left the islands
in search
of new knowledge.
During this travel,
across bodies of water
they were
separated
from eachother

returning with   new knowledges

stored within   ::   their bodies

                     ::

prior to this, they had always
held knowledge
together,
always together.

There were many things they lost and gained on this journey
the chant

given by women, worn by women,
transformed into
given only to men, by men.

My mother left her island
left Savaii, Samoa, to travel to Niu Sila
the land of milk and honey
She was 24.
                              what knowledge(s) did she find?
                              what splitting occurred within her?

I left when I was 24
left a land where the lines of the border were
firmly drawn signalled by the lapping of waves
I moved to the global place of milk and honey
                              this is Amerikkka baby
for the first-time borderlines were apparent to me.

With this movement
my lines of identity shifted.
For once I knew where I had come from,
I felt that I was standing on firm ground
my internal dialogue finally silent.
Someone asked me the other day
does this place feel like I home?
I responded
                              a version of myself lives here
                              they had their back turned to me
                they immediately looked back, gave me a look,
                                                of recognition.

in the transformation
that occurs in the crossing
in this case across the ocean,
always the ocean
after the crossing,
you can often see
behind you and in front.   >>>
you can see parts of yourself   >>>>>>
that you were not privy to before   <<<   >>>>>>>>>
new names are taken   <<<<<<   >>>>>>
poles of identity planted to recognize   <<<<<<<<<   >>>
these shifts in belonging.   <<<<<<
The ocean is our pathway   <<<
she connects
whenever I am greeted by her
I can feel her power
and I know she always remembers me.
you always know when you are near her
you can smell
that sweet,
salty, breath
caressing your skin.
when she greets you at the sami
baptizes you with her cold, invigorating,
salty self
you breathe in her goodness
before submerging yourself again
meeting her and greeting her
over and over

m o a n a

I always know where I come from
when I am greeted with that smell
I know that I am from the ocean
and I will always find my way home
if I follow her   <<<
          <<<<<<
          <<<<<<<<<
m o a n a   <<<<<<
          <<<

she
calls
to

me.

>>>
>>>>>>
>>>>>>>>>
>>>>>>
>>>

Sometimes,
I will check my weather app
and I will see that it is raining here,
in New York and raining
simultaneously
in Auckland.

This duality makes me think of my grandmothers.

I have been seeing this duality everywhere lately.

I like to think the practice of having a soa
honors the duality of the first twins
these aitu,
the first bearers of this knowledge.

Thinking about Taema and Tilafaigā's journey to Fiti*(uta)*
mapping their possible journeys
across islands

S A M O A   F I J I   T O N G A

I trace the letters' physical movement
on my modern tapping tool
and wonder at their apt placement
how this archipelago of keys
mirrors the physical geography
of these sea of islands
so well

S A M O A

F I J I   **O**

A   **N M**

and how they are in relationship with each other
this cartography mimicing the golden triangle

Strokes
keys in time(s)
this, is my navigational tool
a personal mapping made possible.
Like the marks made specific to each navigator
this choreography is specific to my lima and tino.
These are my tender marks
my stories
rendered here
for you
to sit
with.

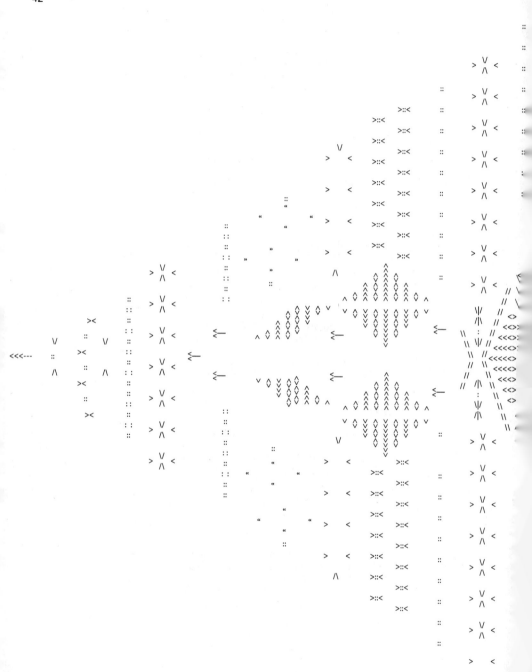

Audrey Brown-Pereira

who are you, where you come from, where you been your ( )hole life?

we grow different   under artificial light

heaters in the winter   we're not allowed to use
                               only hot water bottles
                               and velvet blankets with lions and tigers
                               and duvets and continentals with gardens of flowers

covering us   to keep us warm   in this cold
not in   our blood   only eyes and skin

descendants of shift workers

                               7 am to 4 pm

                                              4 pm to 12 am
clock-in
clock-out
check-in
check-out   and again and again and again

lines of production for

biscuits to drive and cars to eat at takeaways with beer in crates and fish and
chips in newspapers no one reads except for the horses on the radio for the
am and the fm eating meat pies and sausage rolls with tomato sauce and
pig heads and fish heads with blue tin labelled from sāmoa of fresh coconut
cream to cover the banana and pumpkin poke and sides of mainese and
chop suey and fried flounder and crayfish with raro doughnuts buttered with
marmite drinking sachets of powdered juice

villages of suburbs   with buses and factories
                          and farmland   eaten
                                        for cemeteries and highways

                          and airports and all her expansions
                          against a changing sky and sea where the land
                                  shift work
                                        stop work
                                        no work   redundancies

and   unemployment
and   benefits   your worldview
                                                not tall
                                                but huge with clear eyes
                          everywhere brown
south auckland   land of māori and pacific people

                                        few pākehā
                                        here and there
mainly teachers
and people on the tv
                          in   that other world
                                        another new zealand
                                        foreign and out of

                                        reach

intangible

muldoon, lange, palmer, moore, bolger, shipley, and clark
kiwi names in your living room with access to your remote control
look nothing like mum and dad

2022 in transit to depart for europe

looking from inside

        the sitting room   of your childhood

knowing your own children

        don't get you

        don't get it

        don't want to   as no need too

being daughters of the i(s)lands   fully sovereign

                                  in their

                                  self

                                  assurance

2022 in transit to return from europe

bare feet on the chinese mat

        neatly covering the carpet

        below the sofa

of embroidered cushions   and family portraits

                wall papered with shell ulas

                and church hats

quilted together

with scent of tiare māori and feijoa

        return to sender

        you gently fold the tivaevae

        you will take home with you

Maringikura Mary Campbell

Dreams

Arita dreams
of super heroes
tough guys fighting
with swords and guns
and stuff . . .
And I dream
of a vaka climbing the ocean
of a whale rolling under
and I wonder
could I ride this fish?

Savaiki

Born of Te Ariki
Descended from
Atea and Hakaotu
Do not judge me
because my skin burns in the sun
I know who I am
and the direction I am travelling
Towards Savaiki
Towards the Son

Denise Carter-Bennett

Hēninuka

My kūpuna Hēninuka
Hair dark and wavy,
Tongue accented with Oʻahu
A child of only 17
With babe in arms and husband away
In a foreign land but not foreign at all
Kuia cradling you while you cradle your own
Faces that remind you of your ʻohana but tikanga
not of your own
Kūpuna, tūpuna, tīpuna
You share the same
Waka hourua made a home here
Your canoe to this foreign place was cold,
destitute, unwelcoming
Your husband with his alabaster skin and Yiddish ways
Your belly swollen with the ache of love forbidden
Jane is what I will call myself. My husband will call himself John.
Kāo. Hēninuka. HĒNI
The kuia say you are one of us
Kūpuna, tūpuna, tīpuna
We share the same

Hone, you shall call him Hone
This child of yours hair dark and wavy
Skin like alabaster but golden when loved by
Tama-Nui-Te-Rā
Why does he sound like one of those haole?
His reo speckled with Oʻahu and tangata whenua
He's going to marry a Māori girl
A chief's daughter
Her hair dark and wavy

Her skin golden like Rā
Her reo haole, tangata whenua, mātauranga
Māori, love
Kūpuna, tūpuna, tīpuna
They are the same

You see her in your dreams
This child of 17
Her dark and wavy
Her skin golden for Rā
You reach out but space and time deny it
She sits there drowning in her darkness
Crying out for Hinenuitepō
Screaming out for Rohe
Oh sweet Moko, I am here to cradle you
Do not jump off!
Ra'iātea is not ready
Your tiare apetahi still forming
Her reo filled with pain and whakamā
I AM NOT MĀORI she spits out
Kānaka, Māori, kaikamahine Moana is who you are
Fiery like Pele, born of her
You weave a kete of aroha, discovery and acceptance
You put it on a waka hourua and set it out onto the moana
Over time and space it will reach her
Kūpuna, tūpuna, tīpuna
I am her and she is me.

Emalani Case

On Being Indigenous in a Global Pandemic

In a global pandemic,
being Indigenous means
the words,
'we're all in this together',
don't really apply to you
because we're not really

all in this together,
not when some of us
have to protect ourselves
and our families
from disease, disappearance,
and disregard

from the threat of war games,
of 25,000 personnel
converging in your waters,
on your land,
promising security,
while putting you at risk,

the military rhetoric really saying,
we're willing to kill you
to save

some

from the threat of infected sailors,
disembarking an infected ship,
staying in hotels,
breaking quarantine rules,

forcing Guåhan to choose,
who to give beds to,

the navy rhetoric really saying,
we have one-third of your island;
we want two-thirds

more

from the threat of construction
on burial sites,
a greedy mayor calling
for non-essential work,
and protectors arriving
in masks, social distancing
from the living, not the dead

the political rhetoric really saying,
pandemic or not, alive or not,
you're still not

worthy

not worthy
of the same protection
extended to some
not extended
to you

because in a global pandemic,
being Indigenous
is like every other day,
struggling to be seen,
only now from

isolation

In a global pandemic,
being Indigenous means

protecting land
when you can't stand on it,

protecting people
when you can't hold their hands,

protecting yourself
when you can't rest,

or take long quarantine naps like others because

colonialism,
capitalism,
militarism,
and racism

are not resting
but working overtime

In a global pandemic
being Indigenous means

waking up realizing,
we've been here before:
ancestral memories
swirling in your veins

corrupt captains
so-called discoverers,

preaching salvation,
bringing disease,

your heartbeats
leaping from your chest
to resuscitate
generations

then
now
and
not yet born

In a global pandemic
being Indigenous
means even the word
'lockdown'
is misplaced
because it implies

we all had the same
freedoms to begin with,

we all have the same resources
to entertain and sustain,

we are all somehow 'jailed',
facing a common enemy

that still impacts
disproportionately

In a global pandemic
being Indigenous means

even this poem
will be attacked
and its author called

insensitive
for wanting to talk about injustice
in a time of global death,

privileged
for having the energy to complain
in a time of global death,

cruel
for cultivating cynicism
in a time of global death,

and maybe even lonely
for retreating to words
in a time of global death

But in a global pandemic
being Indigenous means
writing,
speaking,
crying,
and protesting

your people into existence

because in a global pandemic
being Indigenous means
the very forces
that try to assure you that
'we're all in this together'

are the same forces
that will make the 'new norm'
an extension of the old:
a world where being Indigenous
means still having to prove

we're here

Hele Christopher-Ikimotu
Dear Banaba

I already know the pain of losing my island
They say never forgive and forget
But how can I forgive a man for destroying land I will never get to walk on?
How can I forgive man for digging up the resting home of my ancestors?
How can I forgive man for stealing a part of my identity before I was even born?

Dear Banaba,
I will never forget you
Your blood and sweat nourished the land I currently live on
You died so I could live

I wish people knew about you
Maybe then the world would care about losing their home
Not just to the waves and the changing climate
But to man

Will I lose my other islands the way I lost you?
To corporate greed, injustice and carelessness for the environment?
Will my future children and grandchildren lose their identity before they're born?
Will they ever get to walk on the land of their bloodline?
Will there even be a place for them to dig and lay me to rest?

Will they forgive and forget?
Because I sure haven't

Unknown

She waits in the cold dark night
Her porcelain skin glimmers
The street light tells her she's beautiful
Adding emphasis onto her petite frame
And eyes of hidden fear
Her shadow creeps behind her
Wishing they were in control
Wishing their human form would just walk away
Wishing they weren't camouflaged with the surrounding darkness
I, shrouded in the confines of a safe environment
Ears entertained with soothing melodies
She, with passing pupils plastering themselves onto her fragile body
Her ears bleeding with torturous definitions
I, with warmth embracing every part of my skin
Heart weeping as hope is created for her with the outcome of rejection
She, with the thin air whispering exploitation onto her bare chest
Mockery invites itself
Parking next to her silhouetted income
Burns her purse with an uproar of laughter
She will take it no more
Her fist introduces itself to their hatred
They leave her home
Her road
K road
Evil road
Sad road
Only road which makes her feel valid

She flirts with the enemies
Flirts with the enemies
Flirts with the enemies

Beep
Beep
Beep
The sound of her high heels
click,
click
click

As she approaches the tinted window of her master
Ready to be a victim of the unknown
Arrives in a concealed room of sin
Her body, now being used as if it was a commodity of trade
A silent tear runs down her cheek as her comfort zone is stripped
She inhales his intoxicated breath of infidelity
Her vision becomes blurred as she fakes pleasure and satisfaction
She zones out, the sound of the clock drowning in her ear drums
tick tock
tick tock
tick tock
tick tock
And when he's done
He opens his wallet
And closes her legs

She waits in the cold dark night

Gina Cole

His Majesty O'Keefe
(Fitting reflections on a Hollywood movie)

In 1952 they use us as a backdrop
Re-taking, re-staging, re-casting
Writers, directors, camera operators, wardrobe, set design
Re-inventing ways to shoot us
for their settled audiences
Re-arranging our sea of islands to fit their screenplay

This time they send Burt Lancaster
white shirt copra trader
And his infantilised Hollywood bride
Joan Rice, from the trading post in Palau
In the deep background walks a forbidden Fijian Adi
She is fit!

Burt takes Yap rai stones
Gigantic coins of carved polystyrene rock
Wagon wheel size against a coconut tree
On the shores of Culanuku village
Our grandmothers told us the backstory
These fake stones don't fit in our village

An actor from Burma cast as a Fijian medicine man
Blackened eyes sink into made-up Burmese skin
His wrinkled torso, caved-in chest, back-combed afro wig
He stands next to muscled village warriors
Shrinking into place
He is no Fijian, he doesn't fit there

Bully Hayes wanders aimlessly on set, learning his lines
My ancestors keep watch, guarding their red-headed mokos, Bully's mokos

Burt's scene with the Jamaican/Fijian Princess
The ancestors laugh behind their hands
A grab bag of Pacific pick and mix
We are shoehorned to fit a Hollywood construction of us

A patchwork invention for the movie audience
Catching at their colonial feet
We the descendants glance sideways at this myth making
Our aunties are stunt women
The rampage spectacle is too close
We won't let it fit

If you listen very carefully you will hear the Fijian language
Uttering from the lips of Kai Valagi movie stars
The insight of my ancestors teaching them formal dialect
A deep cadence filters from the past
Sa rairai vinaka edaidai
My ancestors' language, my language, fits anywhere

And my bubu, a background extra, exiting a burning bure
Holding a child's hand, her fiery eyes immortalised in film
I can see her at one hour nine minutes and eight seconds
I am following her, I am a background extra
this is my grandmother's village
This is where we fit.

Movie goers in imperial London moon over Burt and the Princess
The village sits with my grandmother in a movie theatre in Suva
Pointing at the screen
Howling with laughter
Dark matinees fill with our language, our light
Our islands
This is where we fit

David Eggleton

Flying In, Southside

At Māngere the airport welcomes you to Middle Earth,
coasting on a jet's wing and a karakia,
but the industrial parkland unfolds as generic,
though 'nesian mystics harmonise snatches of melody
on Bader Drive by the fale-style churches of Little Tonga,
all the way round the Town Centre to busy Pak'NSave,
from whose carpark the Mountain looks back, submerging.

Manaia sail across blue heaven to catch day-dreams;
they glide like slo-mo fa'afafine above South Auckland:
the big box stores, all in orange green yellow or red,
as big as aircraft hangars in this polycotton lavalava
wraparound hibiscus paradise of Pap'toe, 'Tara, Otahu —
the happy coin marts, the fly-by-night clearance outlets,
the stack 'em high, sell 'em cheap, plastic whatnot bins.

A pearl nacre overcasts closed abattoirs of Southdown,
colonial headquarters of Hellaby's meat empire,
shunting yards of Otahuhu Railway Workshops.
Two-dollar leis sway outside shops on Great South Road.
There's Fiji-style goat curry and Bollywood on screens,
kava, taro, fish heads on ice, hands of green bananas —
no sign of Sigatoka blight amid tart tangelo pyramids.

The suburban origami of bungalow roofs is folded over,
under the warmth of 'Māngere'/'lazy wind': so hot and slow
it barely moves the washing on thousands of clotheslines.
Planes touch down; sirens yammer through the tail-backs;
Macca's golden arches sweat the small hours,
and a police chopper after midnight bugs the sky;
weaving back and forth over quiet streets of Manurewa.

The Great Wave

There is no god but God, go mongooses in the monsoon.
The rains thrum on empty biscuit tin drums
to rattle Suva market and flick your face.
The jail's walls are ivory; a rainbow crooks an elbow.
The old shoeshine boy begs for money
for a cup of tea and two pieces of bread.
Everybody wears jogging shoes and sneakers,
the jingle-jangle of the bangle-seller is drowned
by a radio that could walk five hundred miles,
and then go walking on the moon to a bass line by Sting.
A crimson hibiscus lei drapes the punchbowl
at the bar, where I renovate my inner temple
and wait for the night to extend my winning streak,
as hotel staff slice tops off fresh pineapples
to reach garlanded pinnacles of mirrors.
A hinge bends to lift a drift log from the surf.
Thus spake Zarathustra to the fa'afafine:
bruise me with purple shadows of evening fallen
over searched caves of eyes that lids close on.
I listen to the ocean chant words from Rotuma.
The *Mariposa* is a butterfly between islands.
A heatwave, fathoms green, whose light spreads
its coconut oil or ghee or thick candlenut soot,
twinkles like fireflies over plantation gloom,
and heart's surge is the world's deep breath.
I learn to love every move the great wave makes;
it coils you into each silken twist of foam,
blown far, all the way to salt-touched Tonga,
with mango pits, wooden baler, shells awash.
My uncle, swimming from New Zealand, wades
out of the sea and wades onshore at Levuka,

where my grandmother is staring out
from her hillside grove of trees waiting for him.

Lifting the Island

Virtuous sunlight lifts the island to prayer.
The abyss is dizzyingly blue to dive into.
Surfers are carried on the backs of waves.
Hotels rear balcony totems notched skyward.
Heat yawns with a reptile's tranced shimmer.
Dazzled clouds somersault; then roll away,
from a day flapping in an ocean breeze.

Girls in just bikinis and flip-flops,
their long hair streaming in the wind,
weave mopeds and surfboards beachwards,
listening to iTunes, white buds in their ears,
flat out in heavy traffic, as fat men
on fatter hogs roar along with the racket
of low-flying, propeller-driven, fighter planes.

The beachcomber who once sailed seven seas,
goes from bin to bin with freestyle hands,
grave as a mandarin in abstract thought.
Ripe stink of garbage. Hot weeks of August.
He wears nothing but faded and ripped shorts,
his muscles ripple under sun-blackened skin,
his fingers toil to free mashed drink cans.

The old gods are curios, remade in the bar
as the grinning wooden handles of beer taps.
Those at the bar, heads bowed, dream of surf,
dream of white foam swept into a cold glass.
Fleeting moments woven like flower garlands,
a seaweed hula undulating in a ship's wake.
The howl of air-con strains to cool down rooms.

Catch the smoking wave on winged heels,
orchidaceous comber that lifts rose-gold,
before deep green, light green, greener, bluer,
deeper, darker, roller-slider rising, standing,
before weight of water beneath the standing
wave topples to wipe out, because the sea
has been stopped by land shelving beneath.

Amber Esau

Liminal

Parted down the middle, his sharpened cuerpo
struts out of a waspish cave in the dark

harakeke, strands bowing under a nosey tūī
eyeing the red beaned flower that's claw-like

in lazy light. We lock eyes in glass. Feathers
and flax. He stares from corners acting coy

but this is k'rd, bruh, a Queen will call you
out for not looking long enough. I ruffle

the curls searching silences in the glare
knowing? Not quite slow moving but watchful

the manu drops a beak at onyx arrowhead
eyes forgetting forward. Down the vague grey

he walks the tūī across the winking glass
into a powdery afternoon, kicking up silent

dust behind them on the street. They swoop to the top
of St. Kevin's perched for a second before flying off

into the blue thin as the moon of pulotu
dragging nails across the fog and Paz.

Street Fighter

Just past the gate the footpath's a cloud squeezed out like tea towels
Mum hangs in the
morning, eh? Dark
and splotchy as ants walking Nutella sandwiches with crusts cut off
flattened into benches all along the tech block. We pretend to listen to
the teacher's last reminders over the bell.

Once we throw the ringing behind us it's hop
skip

and jump the cracks with zig-zag weeds and Roman sandals
and ew
toes
but we
'bout to walk home with mates now, might as well be adults —
and ew
crooked lines
and we
'bout to walk near some sun now, it's wagged the whole day —
nah, ew
keep the count
and don't step on odds or else you're out.
Cars dribble past us like baby vom —
nothing
then
blues as
we get spat on
by headlights
and hide it from the rain.

The bell's already gone two minutes of a day too crunch-soggy and woah

yep

still so muggy we're rushing forward
some cars reverse
keep driving, creeps, keep driving
they're honking big as a hadouken and quick as one, too, quicker than
the fingers we pull behind them. Keep driving, creeps, we whisper 'til
they leave, then shout.

The cement's about to rain, just, not at the dairy
a ring of school uniforms tightens like a scrunchie
a dark blue shelter covers the five-second walk to the spacies
just outside the shop door.

Some say our hands are so dainty they'll swat us away and we're mad
but quiet with it since our cousin's up soon and he'll own the winner, easy.

We squeeze past inside pick out the ten-cent lollies we'll scoff before
getting back.

That's old-school, bro. That's no charger styles, eh?
counting coins out onto the counter a tinny knock by the two-dollar bags
of snakes and marshies

standing tall surrounded by a few kids in our year and two oldies in high
school uniform vs-ing each other

red and blue
Ken and Ryu
we only had $3.50
but that'll fill a bag with rabbits when our new magic trick is learning to
want and want to change the metal to mallow they go

down down left

     and up right left

   and down left third button mash

watching the fight from the shoulders and the down diagonal forward
punch so everyone oohs and ahhhs in the light at the end of their fists

for the rest of the walk home.
Like seagulls, some of the kids flap closer to us lollies clutched in our

fists they ask for some we laugh and sing

nah, bro!
past all the picket fences
nah, bro!
come play spacies then! they shout
nah, bro!
Laughing
 out of breath at the end of the street already swapping lollies between us
                      just a left right down 'til home
power walking to make sure we're on time to pull the washing off the line
before Mum wakes up for the night shift
shoving lollies
all the way home.

Sisilia Eteuati
Denial

They say diabetes is a silent killer
a thief in the night
that creeps up to you like a moetolo
embracing you against your will

but I saw him coming
in the WTO siusiu pipi and mamoe
and 5 cans of coke I had

before lunch

I saw him coming
but in my Samoan pride
I scoffed

laughed like it was a fale aitu

and said

aga ou te le fefe i le oti.

They say diabetes is a silent killer
so we don't say much about him
as we shovel suka into our koko alaisa
and sneak off to shove a needle in our stomach

and when he strikes

and takes my eyes
            my teeth
                  my legs

I will say

the Lord works in mysterious ways

and be praised

for my faith.

Postscript

I wrote this poem after being inspired by Sia Figiel's bravery in speaking out about her very personal struggle with diabetes. It showed me how we all have to speak out because our Pacific health statistics are a tragedy. It also showed me that I have to take action to not be one of them.

Island Girl

I once wore a shirt
That had 'island girl
fresh and sweet'

emblazoned
in bright yellow
across it

the words shaped
into a pineapple

and I

who was neither
fresh nor sweet

enjoyed the irony

Now I live
in Auckland

and in winter

I buy pineapples

all the way from the Philippines
for $3.78

and hope
the distance
they have travelled

hasn't soured them.

Niusila Faamanatu-Eteuati

For the learners of Gagana Sāmoa —
O se faʻamanatu mai le Matāmatagi

A taili le matagi i suiga ona popoʻe lea o le tōfā
A faʻataʻutaʻu le laʻi pe matagitogaina ona fetuʻunaʻi lea o le lā
A siʻisʻii le gataifale ma souā le fogātai ona sisi lea o le lāʻafa
Le lā fala i le agi fīsaga po o le matāʻupolu nai le atuvasa
Tautai tu i le foe, mataʻalia faʻatonufolau, le tapasā lenā
Neʻi lōfia i le tuʻāoloa, pe sasi au taga e toe tau tatā
Tagoʻau i au measina, o lau gagana e oʻo oʻo ifo i le loto
Na te faʻatupu ma faʻa ʻoaina lagona, logoitino, ivi ma le toto.
Utugāʻoamau ia lē tūfalaʻaia tupulaga mo le lumanaʻi
Tatou umufonotalatala, matimati le gagana, o se
Faʻamanatu mai le Matāmatagi.

Unfathomable insight is dubious in times of swirling storms
Adjusting the sail when destructive southerlies blow
When facing storm surges and rough tides, raise the sennit sail.
While the easterlies gust with the woven mast on calm seas
The navigator at the helm, the sturdiest in steering and forecasting
To rise above the strong northerlies and unexpected difficulties
Holdfast to your treasures, your language speaks to the hearts
It soothes the soul, felt by your body and sensed by your bones and blood
Charging the funds of knowledge for future youth, ensuring no one is
left behind
Let us engage in deeper conversations, revitalise the language, a
reminder from Matāmatagi.
Because every heritage language thrives within steadfastness and
affirmation.
If well nurtured in the homegrown, it survives and blossoms in the
peripheral

Aigagalefili 'Fili' Fepulea'i-Tapua'i
275 Love Letters to Southside

Auckland is not the same place as South Auckland.
When I learnt that no place outside of South Auckland would want to
pronounce my name properly
I scraped it off their tongues
So now all they do is spit on us instead
And still.
Haven't my ancestors' screams been muffled between textbook pages?
Didn't a white teacher at my South Auckland sch tell us we're just
'typical South Auckland crap'?
Aren't I lucky I wasn't born when the dawns were raided?
Still.
My South Auckland
Red and blue runs through your streets in the forms of bandanas, flags
and flashing lights
So much that everyone chooses to forget what the colour of our sun
looks like.
Chooses to see the negative rather than what shines more bright.
Shine flashlights in our brown boys' eyes so much
That I can never forget what the colour of our sons looks like.
While our daughters become mothers to their siblings so young because
their parents work shifts at night.
The media won't talk about that but will focus on any recorded street fight.
Everyone loves to quickly point fingers but no one can afford the time to
ask why?
I've lived my life growing up in classes where I had more friends with no
lunch than friends who were eating
I've heard my friends say 'they growl us for not having laptops when we
barely have lunch' more times than I've heard a school bell.
Joking about your pain is a right of passage in South Auckland schools
Because it's not like these education systems teach us how to deal with it.
And still,

Isn't the reality of our lives to you just politics?
And ever since Ponsonby left my mother for a white woman
I noticed that any door I walk through outside of Southside lacks a
welcoming mat.
Driving through Ponsonby is looking at collections of faded photos I
don't remember living through.
It is the movie I never got to watch.
A chance of a happier brown community is just another one of its
deleted scenes.
Ponsonby is your cousin that forgot their roots so their branches grew
away from us
But in Southside family is still family
So when Ponsonby shows up uninvited to the family function I will
awkwardly kiss their cheek.
Wait for them to tell me I am a splitting image of my mother
But they never do.
And still.
I could stand here and offer all the reasons I love my home as a peace
offering.
Try to pull the moana out of my lungs so I can breathe easier.
Drop my slang and fix my posture.
Make you feel all kinds of ways while I stand here.
But if you saw me on TV?
If you drove past me on my streets?
Aren't I just a little brown girl from South Auckland?
Still.

Maureen Mariner Fepuleai
Mum, where are you?

I am organising cupboards;

I am writing to-do lists;

I'm looking inside/outside/underneath and all over the washing machine to find all our missing socks;

I am calculating how to rob Peter to pay Paul so the electricity is not cut off tomorrow;

I am putting away clean dishes that have been on artistic display on the dish rack for the past week and a half;

I am rushing to go to the toilet before your baby brother screams his head off because he can't see me;

I am counting the coins in the car to make enough money for a 99c high-top loaf of bread from the Otara bakery;

I am replacing the toilet roll that I've shown you a hundred times how to;

I am sweeping up the crumbs you missed under the table, again;

I am swapping out the bathroom lightbulb to use in the kitchen and the bedroom because we can't afford to buy any spares;

I am making something for your class shared lunch today that you only told me about this morning;

I am smiling through my tears when the vices in my head remind me how ugly, how fat, how stupid I am;

I am emailing the school about your lost school jumper, again;

I am rocking your unwell baby sibling back to sleep for the seventh time tonight;

I am praying that the petrol fumes our van has been running on for 24 hours will last till some money comes in tomorrow night;

I am sellotaping my glasses because they are coming apart;

I am folding the 5-day-old family laundry that has been sitting in the lounge in plain view of everybody;

I am duct-taping the hole in the sole of my shoe so the water doesn't seep in;

I am ironing your school uniform for class photos tomorrow;

I am picking up these lego blocks that I asked you to take care of last night before you went to bed;

I am feeding the damn cat you begged for and promised me you would take care of;

I am stifling my sobs of loneliness in the dark, underneath the worn and holey duvet I received for Christmas many moons ago;

WHERE AM I, YOU DARE TO ASK???

'I am right here baby, what do you need?'

Sunema Fesola'i

Passage to Paradise

Boarding late to capture paradise
In awe of your shores
Bored of city CBDs
Give me your fair shores
Your idyllic island breeze
Your swaying palmed trees
To sample but a minute of your surf
Washing pained existence from suburbia
I would drive for hours to escape cityscape monotony
To exhale your fragrant fresh island waves.

Helen Tau'au Filisi
Mana whenua o Māngere

At school I wasn't taught about the history of Māngere or of mana whenua
I instead learned about the histories of the British Kings and Queens
Captain Cook and his discoveries (later uncoveries)
then at uni of US history of Martin Luther King and the great depression
All this while I lived in Māngere.

It wasn't until many, many years later at Te Wānanga o Aotearoa
that I discovered/uncovered that Māngere was where one of the first Māori
kings resided
and that somewhere in the 1300s — even earlier — Māori waka travelled
through with gardens galore
using navigational and cultivational knowledge passed down through the
ages, living bountifully
All this while I studied in Māngere.

Mana whenua graced these lands with plentiful, telling of the story of Hape
and his sacred sites
Long before the 1893 confiscation of lands Act to later resell to the new settlers
The stories of Te Pane o Mataoho and Ihumātao with surrounding mountains
that were then quarried in the 1960s making way for the new airport and roads
and mana whenua could travel to Puketutu Island no more
I learned this whilst I taught in Māngere.

We honour you as mana whenua, a proud people who hold mana and have a
rich heritage
who now act against further travesties of land with encroaching developers,
a new confiscation
Threatening the sacred stories, sacred sites, the very legacy of future
generations
to make way for new housing developments
then mana whenua will see no more
All this while I lived in Māngere.

Kalisolaite Fonongaloa

Untitled

Tall, sky tower ta'ahine,
Crazy, buff netball player,
Mumbling chatter boxer,
Victoria cherry blossom,
Coconut oil tau'olunga.

Tere Takurangi Kathy Ford

New Shoes

'I need some new shoes, can you get me a pair?'
'We got no money my girl', was often the response.
'You are poor, you are poor', 'you got ugly shoes you got ugly shoes'.
A song sung to me because my shoes were hand me downs.

'Your hair smells, your hair smells'.

'Why does your hair always smell like coconuts', the taunting continued.

Another day, another song.
Why did you always put that in my hair?
Could this be why they all get up and walk away when I sit down at lunch?
I need some new shoes, why can't you just get me a pair?

I hate all the songs, not familiar to me.
My Mum sung sweet songs that put me to sleep.
But these songs at school always make me weep.
Hiding in the toilets becomes normality for me.

Finally some new shoes, they didn't last long, now someone else got them on.

Tim Gray

Homeless of the heart

Immense pride
like that
I have of the ABs
winning their (back-to-back,
third time,
away from home)
2015 RWC title,
stops me
from
lying around on K' Rd   or Queen Street
during the day   amongst
the hustle and bustle   . . .   of people going places
mine's a different kind
I choose
anonymity
being a
self-diagnosed
clinically depressed
confined person,
living in the
Ivory Towers
of 4K/16   Chapman Street
homelessness concealing
itself, in the
Newton/Arch Hill
street-side rooms,
so that,
when everyone's
gone for the day,
I lie on my   back-soaked
(circumstance-mattress),   pissed-stained-wetness

delaying yet   another opportunity
to turn it around

Rob Hack

Despite Meena

Despite Meena's temper and rhubarb politics
there is hibiscus to yell its colour at passers by
Manihiki's black pearls and Maungatea to climb.

Despite Tom Davis gone the Sheraton money
gone there are rich fields of taro the reef roars
assurance all day and Mike Tavioni sculpting.

Despite imports Takitimu's bad luck and too
many cars there's Kauraka's stories movies on
at the Empire and market day raw fish and rukau.

Despite talking to strangers about loans plane fares
going up and sons not for the return home there is a
song at the airport Trader Jacks and Emily's t-shirts.

Cannons Creek Four Square

It is tea time the wind is cold and hard I run
head down up Champion Street
two things to remember two things to get
Small tin of peaches, half pint of cream, don't forget.
Then the lights of the Four Square store.
Inside lolly bags hang in rows. In the cabinet
blackberries and raspberries, licorice straps
gob stoppers two for threepence. In my hand hot
with holding a florin and a sixpence. If I get
a quarter pint of cream there'll be money left over.
I fiddle with the money in my pocket, look
up at the lolly bags, then a man with a
badge stands in front of me looking down
What are you hiding in here mister?
He jerks open my raincoat a button flies off
I go backward and forward in his hands he
searches my pockets pulls the coat this way and that.
He huffs, walks away, rubs his hands together
chilly out there isn't it? to a lady coming in.

Outside it is cold. I stand for a long time
tuck in the coat where the button's gone.
I walk home. Mum is taking plates out of
a cupboard, *What took you so long where
are the peaches? What's the matter?*
She bangs the plates down. I tell her and
put the money on the bench. It sticks to
my hand. She pulls out the tucked in part
of the coat where the button was, her eyes
go big she yanks the knife and fork drawer
out, it crashes on the floor. Snatches up the

rolling pin marches to the front door yells
Dad's name twice. He runs after her. My
brothers are now beside me in the hall.
Voices outside. We go upstairs to our bedroom
turn on the light, sit on the bunks.
The front door closes. The knife and fork drawer
is put back. Footsteps on the stairs, Dad comes
into the room, *'It'll be alright'* he rubs my
head and gives all of us a lifesaver.

All day on Ma'uke

All day the reef argues with the sea and no dogs bark.
Palm fronds fall across the road where
goats tied with rope bleat
and pigs scatter through tall grass.

Low cliffs, sand tracks, empty beaches
where tides wash in over the coral shelf
leaving coke cans, plastic bottles, a red jandal.

All day diesel engines hum beside empty drums
coconuts fall, someone on a scooter waves.

All day churches are empty and perfect.
Outside, grey graves sink into the soil
like low lying islands in the sea.

On the roofs of abandoned homes rust spreads.
School kids at keyboards see a future elsewhere.

Grace Iwashita-Taylor
Dear South Auckland

you   beautiful   wild   thing
you are not the comments section of news articles
full of tired assumptions
written by the hands of lazy reporters
whose feet have never walked our streets

you are not the epi-centre of destruction
you are not a hurricane of false narratives

Dear South Auckland Pasifika family
it's not your fault
only healing for you
to drown out the false speakers

South Auckland
you are the womb of creatives
for those that mend
and relentless advocates
of teachers that disrupt the system
and academics that flipped the status quo
a home for parents doing double shifts
from villages that had to become their own eco-system

South Auckland
you are playgrounds that are never empty
and the best place to buy taro
the home away from home
for children of the Moana
we flock to you when we need to remember our roots

South Auckland
my first home after my mother's belly
South Auckland
you know who you really are
South Auckland
you straighten that spine of resilience
and speak

Queen Street Stroll

From the nape of her neck
Queen Street
is looking fine
I stroll down
past the howling builders
I must be lady prey 96 of the day
in Myers Park
Haunted voices of killed beggars
chase me down to Christmas in Aotea Square
Grit-Girls in cut-off jeans
smoke an *I don't give a shit ciggy*
oh . . . but how they do
Policemen on bikes
'bro-talk' a brown ladies temper sideways
A man in a UNICEF t-shirt throws a smile my way
The usual gang of Cut Above misfits crowd the sidewalk
given keys by John to be in engaged activity
with fresh cuts & colours
A young brown woman
sitting next to a diamonds store
asks for change
A brut smelling suit
burns lust through his sunglasses
rubbing up accidentally on young female flesh
In front of the bus depot
a young man asks me if I want free ice cream

Inside the belly of Britomart
a lady pushes a baby
on a pillow in a hollowed-out pram
he has scars from scabs

she wears the WINZ benefit
around her neck
like a ball and chain
It's a bitter late night
and her baby
has no covers on his fingers, toes and head
people stare but never speak

Tinā | Mother

hissing glass laughs
slap her face
as the gods throw stones at her empty bucket
her arms house voices
full fat as horses' veins
bulging rock solid
she presses her feet
deep into the bloody grass
soaking up the crosses of fallen men
a storm of a woman

my mother married her malu alone
I was too afraid to witness
tap tap
blood ink
when I returned home
she lay healing
bloody pillows soaking up the tufuga work
we take her to dip
freshly carved into the mouth of Maraetai
soaking salts to cuts
returning blood back to the vasa
I should have been the vasa

they say ancestors dance on her skin
when she siva Samoa
they say she moves the old way
makes Tagaloa beg for more
the vasa reminisce
and seeds absorb
when she siva Samoa
she dances on ancestors' skin

Caitlin Jenkins
South

our streets grow tread marks in the pattern of tapa cloth,
the men in blue roam them recreating
Da Vinci —
bronze skin mona lisa.
who knew your last supper would be a $2.50 Big Ben pie and a bottle of
stars —
will we ever breathe the same freedom
as our brothers north and west?
cause oceania's waves feel a little too familiar in the backseat
gps broken cause somehow it only circles round these streets —
south,
you are but a direction on auckland's map,
folded tightly into the plastic corners of
red and blue led lights,
police siren jams but not the jawsh 685 type
. . . forever branded as the bottom
the south of new zealand . . .
but it's okay,
we'll tau'olunga on their disrespect
wake them up at dawn with our cheehoos
breathe a brown colour palette back into their colourless minds
love us enough to not need it from anyone else
grow with each other
be strong with each other
block out their white noise with white noise
fill the cracks of Aotearoa's pavements with more reasons to love
south . . .
and put us back on the map . . .
unfold us out of the plastic corners of red and blue led lights
help reverse the damage of our roots with the healing of our new
generations

cause leaves still bloom even more beautiful after the fall
for when our streets grow tread marks
we'll repaint them with coconut oil and fala paongo,
when the world wants our faces to kiss the concrete
we'll still be safe in the arms of papatuanuku
cause when things go south —
we'll deal with them like south —
with the love our roots nourish us in . . .
bronze skin mona lisa,
who knew your last supper would be a feast of the colonised minds . . .
undo the bleaching of your brown colour palette
refill them with all shades of you
cause no direction will define where we're really from,
south

Simone Kaho

...young families, with children.

The overnight rain stops before I wake up and go walking. A blue ball is sitting in wet grass; kids live around here. It matches your eyes and the dress I want to wear tonight but I need to buy it first.

Jasmine is choking out the natives in the creek under the bridge down the street where we used to hang out and look at the naked lady painted on the tree trunk, which also looked like a devil's head on some angles. Her outstretched arms, horns, and her crotch a pointy chin.

She's gone now, and the trunk has split in two, although the tree is still alive. Half the trunk has sent out thin branches that quiver like whips in the morning chill.

Everyone I love has died in one way or another but it's spring.

I died too, to make way for something new, and we can call it spring. Blossoms swimming in the veins of trees all winter are emerging.

My neck still needs a scarf, but the most tender petals are out, white and pink like little girls' faces. In the kōwhai tree, whose branches are the colour of my face, tūī are getting delirious.

I meet an old lady in the Coffee Project getting my almond flat white. She licks her keeper cup and talks about how *the Islanders* moved into Waterview after *the old people* who used to live there *died off*. She says *Islanders* with narrowed eyes and a pause. *Anyway*, she smiles and licks. Spit glints in the air. *It's changed again. Now it's young families, with children.*

Half

An Air New Zealand training manual gets leaked. It says Tongans are softly spoken but drink the bar dry. Maybe it's a Tongan thing, like gold teeth. I'm softly spoken but drink the bar dry and I'm hardly Tongan. Only half. Air New Zealand hosts can't tell when I get on the plane though because my Tongan is not straight down the middle. It's mixed all in, so it looks like something else. Like if you were to mix peanut butter and jam in a glass jar. You get a pink-brown mixture with raspberry pips and nutty bits. Not stripes like the Australian product. That didn't last long on our shelves. There was too much peanut butter in it. The stripes only lasted the first couple of toasts, then after that it was just pink-brown mush in a glass jar. No gold teeth though.

Jam

Sometimes Dad would get out the guitar and sing sad songs and talk about his mum who died of cancer after he came to New Zealand. He played 'I am an Island' and Kenny Rogers, he made up songs for us, one was about bananas. He smelled sweet, I was too young to know it was whiskey. He gave me Mackintosh lollies from his secret inexhaustible stash, and I'd sort them into favourites. I remember smiles maybe some tears. He'd hug me in-between songs. I remember him sitting by the window with orange curtains in the lounge, Simon and Garfunkel records on the ground, his guitar on his knees, afternoon light on his face.

Daren Kamali

Duna does Otara
(South Auckland)

Writing about Otara, aye?
Capital of Polynesia, right?
Music blasts from *Rups Big Bear*
outside *Otara Library*
on the pavement

an eel comes to life
belly slides
through *Otara Town Centre*
its head sways
in admiration
murals on the wall
past *Fresh Art Gallery*
through the *Fale Pasifika*
under the rook of *Ika*
past *ASB Bank*
past the *Post Office*
first stop
Samoa Money Transfer Limited
looks around
hidden cameras
nothing but brown in Otara town
Capital of Polynesia, right?
Duna — slides around the corner
smells
greasy fast food
takeaways — bakeries — dairies
past the alcohol store
not good for the heart
all run by Chinese and Indians

Capital of Polynesia, right?
as he passes the *TAB*
in the corner of his eye
across the road
he spots the *Diabetes Project Trust*
beside the Otara Police Station
last stop
Parkinson and Bouskill Headstones
beside the children's playground
Duna is now depressed
too long has he seen
broken promises and dreams
in the **Capital of Polynesia**
Duna slides on
through *Otara Music and Art Centre*
past murals on the wall
past *Fresh Art Gallery*
back to his spot — in the concrete
outside *Otara Library*
Capital of Polynesia . . . RIGHT

Coconuts don't grow here

Coconuts sleep on cardboard boxes
Frozen ground and rock-hard pillow

Coconuts grow tall like the Sky Tower
Carried away by the pokie machines

Coconuts dream in colours
Blinded by neon lights and 99 lovers

There's nowhere to sleep in the city
Only vacant emergency housing
Where no one wants to sleep
Even during covid

They take to the streets

Coconuts cross the ocean floor
Island to island

They are immigrants to this whenua
Visitors coming to cold jungle concrete
Ancestral stories told to city pigeons

Arriving fresh and vibrant —
To build Tāmaki Makaurau

They were moved to Ōtara
And South Auckland

They float aimlessley through the city
Growing into foreign tongues

From spirit houses —
To red-light district

User pays in the Big Bad City
Strays pray in the Big Bad City

Coconuts get around the city
On the sidewalk with a plastic cup

They pay attention to garbage bins and loose coins

A coconut feeds birds with
Leftover chips from a stranger

Coconuts grow to forget their motherland
Forget their roots — language and culture

Forget to remember
How far they've drifted from home

The city does not want a drifting coconut —
Does not care for him at all

Coconuts don't grow here.

Manteress

Flying
      into the depths
            of the underwater world
wings spread out
      as she rides
            underwater tides
Confident and playful
      grin on her face
            stars in her eyes
                lips
      red as hibiscus
            She chants juicy mango melodies
                performing na meke ni yalo
            Ni sa Bula
      she calls to the giant
Manteress:
            Curu I tuba kuita mai qito
come out of your dark hole squid and play
                follow me to my side of the ocean
            Out of the abyss
Kuita: Ocei o iko? — who are you?
          O Au o Marama Vai
            I am Manteress
goddess of the sea
      curious to see Kuita's full form
chanting: Mokosoi oi lei
            seducing him out
Kuita stunned — thinks:
Who dares come close?
            his head pops out of the cave

Manteress quickly places
                    a lei of shells
over the giant's head
            she swims away
                    towards the underwater currents
Manteress: Muri mai Kuita — follow close squid
                         Kuita is taken back by her charms
            so flamboyant
        so colourful
full of surprise
          she intrigues him
Kuita has roamed the seven seas for centuries
                  never has he seen such a creature like this
                they swim on
Kuita: Kauji au ivei?
            Manteress: Trust me — follow me close
                through the passage in the reef
                    into the harbour
                towards the mouth of the river
never has Kuita come so close to shore before
                up river they swim
                    rocks melting behind them
river disappears into the underworld
                      swallowed by the past
covering the path back
            to his ocean cave
          Manteress calls:
Sega na leqa — Don't worry
          Out of her giant manter-self
                morphing into an island goddess
Kuita cannot believe his eyes
             What has just happened?
So unreal, he blinks in disbelief
          What a sucker for her charms

Kuita transforms into an island man
        tentacles blazing
    bulbous eyes flash
          on savage face
        arms raised to the heavens
            yells Ha!
        to the gods
dreadlocks
      pour
from island hands
    Manteress becomes
       a slender Nesian goddess
         kisses her lover
      embracing him
    in a pool of lava
under the waterfalls
      into the sunset
    she whispers
The Gods of Oceania have spoken
    You are now a man
your name is Teuthis
      Teuthis on land
    Kuita in the sea
He stumbles
    confused over streams
      to a lava pool
        soaking his locks
    contemplating
revelations from the day
    trying to make sense
          of what happened
           thinks too hard
      Am I losing it?
he falls into a deep sleep

wakes to no Teuila by his side
footprints he follows
he follows
    bird
       like
          foot
             prints
running through the forest
    to mountaintop
        I
        am
        Teuila
           flower of Oceania
      Manuvaku of the air
Manteress of the sea
morphing once again
    from island empress to manuvuka

    I am but a messenger
here today — gone tomorrow
    back to the bird of the air
      that I am
    with a backward glance
she leaps off the cliff top
    Teuthis watches her
      disappear in the sunrise
        just as she appeared
    Unannounced
She disappears
    leaving Teuthis
      lost and confused —
    Where to from here?
  cursed to roam
foreign soils for eternity

never will he see

such mysterious trinity

wondrous living being

queen of the wind

Adi of the islands

Goddess of the sea

She is the

unspoken truth of Oceania

Teuthis watches her fly away into the sun.

Mereana Latimer

PLASTIC pēpē PLASTIC

Their teacher's Samoan but they say, *he's vegetarian, came from*
the big city, wanted a lifestyle change. These kids got the internet
to navigate the moana, a hand on the heart of their 'enua
a foot stuck in two front yards. There are instababes now
with long black hair, they eat chop suey now, say
you gotta eat meat to be real.

Your nana got married in the PI church, ran the trams until the family
was a row of houses loving on moon faced weetbix babies
out in Cannons Creek. E pēpē, the island that birthed her is unreal
like a shit-house divorce that got covered up years ago
like an earring you lost and pretend you don't care about
all your IV lines are flavours and your visuals
are Google Maps.

Strangers pick you as Spanish, say *you must be from*
the Middle East, maybe South America, your English is really
good? Welly boys show you they're cultural, they ate pigeon
in Vietnam, smoked some pot out of a hookah, really vibe
with Buddhist energies, wipe you clean
of colonial guilt.

Your nana would say it's good, like strings of yellow plastic beads
draped over polyester floral dresses from the Warehouse.
If you ever wore gold e pēpē, she would yell *take that off*
before someone rips it from you! Because you never know
where the thieves are hiding, even in the hospital wing
at the rest home in Maupuia.

Kristoffer Lavasi'i
What Remains to Be Seen

We wrote ourselves into the spaces they left.
If theirs is a story defined by presence — stark marks in colonial ink
Then ours is defined by absence — the great white vastness
that stretches between period and capital letter.

In their myths of 'New Zealand'
They write of an agricultural centre bursting with life
Watered by distilled heavens, each drop a perfect piece of infinite blue.
They do not write of how their endless eden
was paid in sweat that still soaks the weathered roots
In broken bodies that have become the boughs of a gafa
that never reaches high enough to climb over the fence
In beatings hearts rent from loving islands bodies
to be transplanted into a cavernous ribbed cage,
a defiled mother, an echo chamber with strange white blossoms
that rain from the sky that quench the hearth fire hearts
Crushing the dancing flames of sun-strained island joy into pale
submission — the land of the great white crowd

Their faulty understandings of te-moana-nui-ā-kiwa
saw them craft walls that broke our oceanic highways
They drew arbitrary axes that, before their arrival, had never existed
They ripped out the truth of places, exchanging them for prophecies
composed of child-scrawl scratches scored into a map, a history book, a
piece of legislation
A palimpsest of pain, each report, court decision, health check, 'history' report
overwriting the humble pages of tapa cloth dedicated to the memory of
those who follow after

They wrote off our memories as foolish murmurings
'There is no way that people could deliberately traverse the Pacific'

'There is no way that they could comprehend the complex rhythms of life'
'There is no way they could have sophisticated social structures'

They told us to forget ourselves and so we were made
to abandon our reflections, finding solace in the shadow that forever
trailed in our wake
That precious remnant of ancestral ink tattooing our hearts, indelible
memories printed in steel ink

But some remained, staring deeper into the great inverted sky
a compilation of the currents that moved to the rhythm of ancient memory,
catching the glossy shifts of the future in the ocean's eternal dance
Adhering to the primordial wisdom spoken in the ocean's tongue:

Change comes

We annotated their pages
We referenced their paragraphs and fact checked their reports
We reviewed their numbers
We rewrote their clichés,
Their stereotypes
Their tired old lines
We *killed* their darlings

We wrote ourselves into the spaces they left
In the spaces between the letters, in the silences that spoke of the unsaid

We are done writing their pathetic stories — now . . . now we write our own.

Daisy Lavea-Timo

Fringe Dwellers

If I was to map a settlement narrative that led to my creation
I'd start by saying my heart beats louder than my words
See there's this big, silver teapot of 100% pure
Organic-Superfood-Koko-Samoa bubbling in my stomach
Tooting hunger and obesity through its long nose
in shrill whistles that pierce my insides

The little girl feeling around
Making sense of the terrain
Plays indiscernible chord progressions known only to those
Who stand in the shadows of intersections

When parents bend time to cross only at twilight
She quickly learns how to tuck her siblings
and herself in
into South Auckland Primary school shoes with holes sellotaped whole
and shoes 3 sizes too big as the Head Girl of a decile 10 high school in
Epsom
She, colours outside lines that come together in stark contrast
This, preacher-turned-poet silences in the pulpits of magnanimous
churches

She's too aware of the red lights on all four corners
1. How did you get an A+?
2. You're here on the Pasifika quota right?
3. Can't succeed in one world and can't succeed too much in the other
4. How much do you get an hour?
As if that dollar value = her worth.

Flirting the line
Between humility and arrogance

She negotiates words that divide moments
For expectations' sake

Sitting in the margins and knowing how to hold the vā-spaces
Is a blessing
It is to be both the figure Michelangelo said
Struggled to be free from the raw marble
And a living organism called to function and replicate
It is to hold both the chisel and gene
with clean partitions and clock-wise precisions
It is to own it
To know the confluence and liquid alchemy we have always lived in
Permits us to design complex forms with simple code
As we explore solar systems with the same design principles
We realise that we are both
Nature-inspired design and Design-inspired nature
For us
There is no 'part this' and 'part that'
Only Everything and Everyone
Or nothing at all

Mary Lehuanani
Limu

In Samoa, I ate limu.
My brother took the canoe,
dived into the sea
and collected this kind of seafood
floating in the water.
When he came home
we put the limu in the water
to wash away the salt.
Then we put it on the plate
and ate it without cooking.

Now I eat McDonald's.
It is unhealthy
and makes you fat.

Schaeffer Lemalu

im

im
samoan
lebanese
chinese
scottish
blend

my grandparents
on my fathers side
are full samoan
and half chinese

my mother is half lebanese
half scottish

my parents grew up
in a place they
werent made for

dunedin

made for as in
its cold

but communities form
like a cellar of fine
wine and they make it
their own

some weird part
lots of crossing over with everyone else

we moved to pakuranga
auckland
when i was 6
and all of my

friends growing up
seemed to be a similar mix

no one really knowing
who they really were
only where they lived

and the music tv sports drugs that
everyone
could enjoy together

my youngest sister
is the most
conscious of her heritage
out of my siblings and me

in that shes made more of an
effort to rediscover
all sides best as she can

shes the person in our
family who will probably do all the family tree stuff

you know how theres always someone
divinely chosen to care and take care of
it so that it can be a great retirement
hobby or job or just

whatever u spend most of ur time on
to connect all the dots

a part of me feels ashamed that
i dont identify as strongly as i should

with any piece of the blood pie

my grandma has lived in avondale
since the late 80s
going to church playing housie
at the race track with her friends

wearing white every sunday
my grandfather came from
a village with a beach where

ur only allowed to wear white if you walk along it
my sister honeymooned there

sometimes people speak to me with
a kind of respect or appreciation just

because im not white
but i get uncomfortable with it
im no different to
all my friends
some are white as snow

i guess a lot of younger people
are discovering their pasts
and what it means for their future

thats beautiful

i feel stuck in the splotchy pigments
of michael jacksons face

unsure of who i am now that i know
im who i always was
to begin with

just me

a constantly evolving entity

uninterested in making others feel guilty

for things they didnt do

my white friends have suffered in ways my

ethnic friends havent and vice versa and i feel for them

ie polynesian cultures bond in ways

white people have forgotten to

i was living in devonport last year and huge tongan

communities come over during the summers

hottest weekends

all the food out ub40 and other spirituals playing

groups of children with tshirts wading

out in the water longer than me

id smoke a joint then

float on my back till it turned cold

but id turn around and the kids would still

be in the water

made me smile

anyway

what was the point

oh yeah lots of lonely white guys

hang themselves

no support

no one to talk to

they dont have the emotional intelligence

or intellectual capacity to understand themselves

and seek help

its always been a problem

the christchurch killings

were terrifying

i watched this

de palma film a few weeks before where the terrorist does the same thing live on facebook or

whatever facebook is in the film

dynamo or something

anyway

i went into work

and a new chinese intern new to the country

asked me where the closest

shooting range was

i was a bit concerned

why

are you a hunter

no i just want to learn

how to protect myself

if something like that happens again

oh ah no

you cant carry a gun in nz

guns can shoot deer in the bush

ah ok he said

later i found out that his home had been invaded

the week before in avondale and he was

feeling like he had to take

matters into his own hands

i guess we all had a laugh about it

over lunch because some staff were amazed he didnt know

i think there was a cultural lunch that day

people like the christchurch killer dont disappear

they dont seethe they brew

theyre extremely dedicated and theres a point

they cant turn back which might be a long time

before they meet their true reality face to face

can we stop them

i dont think so

theyre loners who cant integrate

up the levels of human experience

and its the only way they can be heard

maybe a person like that

isnt capable of hating

muslims islam is a complex religion

he cant tear down something he doesnt understand

that makes it more tragic

maybe its a fear of his place being taken over

maybe he feels rage at his lack of understanding the isolation

sending him further and further into a place

where theres only him and everyone

else like that joker film

recently it wasnt a cool sexy heath type

take this time

it was disturbing in a

i cant believe the creme da la creme

villain of all time dipped into

the most hated type of person

on the planet at the moment

the weedy angry white male

with terrible life coping strategies

i guess i loved the performance

it was his time to go daniel day lewis in my left foot

i kinda wished it was set

today tho

i just saw a young de niro

talking in the mirror most of the time

anyway

i knew a guy

who was an up and coming rugby league prospect

tore his ankle and it gave him a permanent limp

he spent years beating

people up at the viaduct

on the weekends his family had to send

him back to sāmoa

but they drink more over there he said

last time we meet he was

heading to afghanistan

with a dead look in his eyes

laughing

my uncle joked with me when i was a teenager

i wouldnt survive a week in the islands

because i didnt understand that over there u share

everything even a cup of water is shared

its not yours its everyones

he used to go over to try and help the men

struggling with alcoholism

sometimes if i think

i can see the bright light of my

own despair and depression beginning to rise like

the sun ill ring a free 0800 hotline

just to hear someone on the other line

listen i like that theyre a complete

stranger and i wont feel judged

by any language i put into

words that come out to say something

that means what it says as im saying it

i always feel better

some small victory toward regulating everything in me

the more offended people become

about being able to talk about anything

openly no matter who what

where you come from

the more people will retreat

like a snails eye being

poked in by a child

dont worry

u can relax im just talking something out

in my head

without the news

and everyone else trying to prove

to the world their saintliness

ive met a few saints before

ive seen dirt being thrown

down to fill their graves

Rex Letoa-Paget

Zapelu Kidz

For Fetūolemoana Tamapeau

we all, move like we got the swell of the pacific flowing inside our skin

we all, high fives, electric slides, one, two steps

we all, big hair don't carryah
throw your hands in the aiiryaah

we all, making crop circles on the dance floor

taking

                  up

                        space

     tonight

          we

  are

             the

    Milky

              Way

we all, *skuxx gods*
we all, stop, drop, and roll
we all, not many if any, not many if any
we all, in the gutter churning butter into diamonds
we all, come break my chains come help me out
we all, nesians are you with me

we all, ancestor prophecies. star dreaming philosophies. anchors for the
metaphysical. bloodlines soaked in holy ritual.
we all, descendants of universe weavers. revolutionary thinkers. wayfinding
teachers. emancipation conceivers. master crafters. visionary artists
we all, academic intellects. freedom fighter architects. political trailblazers.
artistic game changers. effervescent orators. land protectors. ego neglecters.
we all, unbury our tongues, say, come as you are. come heavy with shame.
come soaking in regret. come afraid of the past. come eager to learn.

we all, know the reasons we shrink. the weight of grief. losing to survive.
fighting to thrive.

we all, sculpt our table with ancestor ivory.
we all, smorgasbord our dishes with grass roots wisdom.
we all, centrepiece the knowledge we found digging in our backyards.
we all, pass plates through many hands piled high with helpings of one another.

we all, vine our way to joy.
we all, root ourselves in laughter that lifts the room.
we all, wear smiles that stretch the horizon.
we all, blanket the sun like it belongs to us.
we all, mosaic each other back together.

we all, know this is how we begin.

Luana Leupolu

Aeroplanes

I am up on Dad's shoulders: one leg on either side of his head, both hands wrapped around his chin. We start at the house, and fly past the japanese lantern plant; past the swan plant, with the stripy caterpillars and the cocoons waiting to hatch; down by the big shed, tangles of passionfruit vine cascading down its sides; between the fruit trees and their accompanying scents (lemon, feijoa, apple, peach); we reach the back fence, touch it. There are sheep on the other side, and when we are not running, we count them, but there is no time to do that now: as soon as we tap the fence, Dad whips back around and starts down our route again.

His beard is prickly under my fingers. Sometimes he makes aeroplane noises while he runs, taking each of my arms and spreading them out like wings. I let the sensation of soaring rush over me, the crisp, dusk air surging into my face; I tilt my head upwards, giggling at the thrill of being so high off the ground, bum getting sore from the ride. Our garden, blooming and endless, is a single blur below me as we run, and every time we stop for a break, there are more clues that the day is ending: less and less of the sinking sun, the sky a darker shade of blue; the waft of the pork roast inside, the murmur of the six o'clock news.

A Poem I Didn't Think to Write

it was the shining bougainvillea on the western corner of the rooftop:
its colour, its glow,
its annual summer speech

it was the children who played across the street:
a stream of babble, pierced by the girl's *Simon, you're not allowed!*
when their ball rolled out onto the road;
and the meek one, with the golden skin,
who cried at the same time every afternoon

it was the small dog who whisked about
between the pohutukawa shade and the shallows of the sea
sniffling, snuffling, upturning strange rocks;
unable to understand why we drove all the way out there
to lie still on the sand

it was the boozy january night of his birthday party,
and pressing our left cheek against the cool, silent glass
that overlooked the harbour;

it was the scent of the breeze that filled the house each morning
after she had kissed us goodbye and descended the front steps.

yes, but what bougainvillea? what children?
whose dog? whose birthday?

after who kissed you goodbye and descended the front steps?

it was being:
getting it wrong, then getting it right

Luka Leleiga Lim-Cowley

Straightening Out

Content warning: homophobia, death, violence

Our hair is poetry.
Don't forget this.
Even when
words land in you like wounds
There's a poem here
So I write this to you:

When we were in the falema'i
She asked
Why don't i straighten my hair
put it up
into a bun
like
if you can't straighten
you should hide it   i mean,
hide yourself   i mean,
hide all the non-straight parts
of yourself

to be unstraight
is to be dishevelled
without this
order   to make
tidy   to make
clean   to make
moral   harmonious
beautiful
what else
can you be
but a mess?

straighten the hair
straighten her out
because girls
shouldn't be like that
even straight ones

my brother,
they said,
needs straightening out.
alu ese
the army
go full military
anything's better
than that house

in the falemaʻi
all   watching for,
                fearful of
his line, the line
that straightens out
only in death

do prayers not travel in curves and curls?
bend your curve to the normal
become tangent to the normal
graph recurring ever even, ever straight

yesterday, aunty's funeral:
for the first time
her son
he presented
his family
his children
with their

132

two dads
and two mums
mentioned
his sexuality
out loud
not straight
i was so proud
of my uncle
like a
not parent
like the parent
i am not

in the falema'i
say he needs
straightening out, too
straightening out
this straight rage
and
all you can do is
laugh

maybe cut off the unstraight.
maybe shave off the unstraight.
apply heat. do harm.
maybe dye the unstraight,
maybe die the unstraight,
maybe die unstraight,
be made straight in death, maybe

death to the unstraight

and all the unstraight you hide in you.

amen.

Ruby Rae Lupe Ah-Wai Macomber
Storytelling

Violet travelled over 2000 kilometres
for four days to reach NZ shores.
It took her 93 years to return to Fiji.
Her story is one that refuses to fade from my retina.

*

Violet's Pa has his whisky lined up again, he says,
the little girls will have their own men to take care of them one day.
He was gone by the time Violet began school aged 10.
Violet's Ma waited under the coconut tree,
needle and thread in hand.
Everyone dies waiting.

*

The story travels by foreign tongue,
numerous incomprehensible physical gestures,
a lonely sigh
standing awkwardly
out of place
unwilling to chase the pace of New Zealand.
Violet stands in the kitchen of her
three-bedroom rental.
There is curry on the stove.
There are frangipani tucked behind wispy hair.
Hiram, her husband, sways next to her,
dancing his hands upon delicate skinfolds.
He etches finger circles on the nape of her neck,
beard bristle tickles red cheeks.
Two children at work,

the others won't be home until dinner.
Coffee-stained breath,
Na Vale, Home.

*

He left quietly.
When Violet returned
there was no gravity left in her Kaikohe home.
Window paint peeled
as the walls crumbled and cried.
Her son's skinny frame barely filled the casket.
Tapa cloths cover the walls.
Flower wreaths dress the halls.
Family catches the word by phone call.
In a wheelchair,
she cannot reach her child.
Her bones brittle,
he is lowered into the grave
and he will not grab her hand.

*

The room is 10 square feet,
a quarter of which is occupied by the bathroom.
Violet's new Na Vale.
Bingo Thursday lunch,
New Zealand Woman's delivered weekly
after Sunday communion.
Knobbly fingers turn large-print paperbacks cover to cover.
Only airy-fairy English romances stock the shelves,
Pasifika stories lost
below the ocean's surface.

Her muscles seize with movement,
not a loss of memory.

*

Violet puts down the paperback.
Those stories have been imprinted over the veins in her wrist.
Over and over.
Again and again.
So much has been written over the margins of her stories.
She can no longer read her own writing.
The blue ink against caramel wrists,
smear into the waves that lapped against the shores of her homeland,
the waves that battered the boat across the South Pacific.
Waves goodbye.

*

The next storytellers
will be revolutionaries.
Not conquered by their culture.
They don't have to have the right words,
because the next stories have come from long lines of oppression.
The next stories, voices and lives,
are those we have previously refused to hear.
Their stories told as they tilt their davui shells back to their ears.
Hands spread in the opposite of a fist.

Ole Maiava

Can you see me?

Embrace the pain of a ripped
out belief,
Sown by the silence of our ancestor's grief,
Passed down from line to lined,
Our real history is myth defined.

Oral legends are all we have afoot,
Tapped into our skins with walnut shell soot,
Overshadowed by the western light,
Brought to us in the dead of night.

An insidious veil of deforestation,
That burns our roots through colonization,
What we know is not enough,
Unless its framed in the colonizer's fluff.

Our connection to the earth and sky,
Is the answer to the question,
Why?
Who am I, how should I feel?
A ghost in this life,
I yearn to be real.

Can you see me, do you hear my voice?
Stolen from me, my right to choice,
To choose the path of my tupuna,
To swim free as the yellow finned tuna.

Not to be processed and crammed in a tin,
Blamed for the ills of the world,
Cause of the original sin.

This ember of life within,
Burns in us all,
Be kind to each other, we need to heed the call.

The ancient wave is on the rise,
Our lineage comes together in the seas and skies,
You are me and I am you,
Together for better,
That's what we must do.

Ioana Yule Manoa

History

Inspired by Tomaž Šalamun's poem 'History'

Ioana is a queen
knocked off the checkers by a pawn.
She sleeps by day and walks by night, the nightcrawler,
blue and mysterious.
She is Mystique, shapeshifting, people don't recognise her.
Ioana rides Northland's asphalt waves, splashing tar, carving far.
Sandy to Woolley's, the sharks bite at every corner,
it's a Slice of Life.
She swims with mermaids in the pools and with whales at the bay.
Kaleidoscope beauty.
Extended family holidays are a Slice of Heaven,
singing Dave Dobbyn up the laundry chute.
Playing spies. I spy.
Reading hour is cuzzie hour, is weaving flax flowers,
extended family photos, immediate family photos, in height order, in age order.
She's a Kiwi, a flightless bird, on a school trip to Buenos Aires.
Piso or peso? a friend asks her.
Tango dancers, jewellery merchants and merchandise sellers line la calle.
Fileteado dance the walls,
football heroes cover the halls.
She rips weeds from between the cobblestones,
waits for them to grow again,
shoots for 3s, looks up to Steven Adams
spectating Friday night bball.
Her Kobes are anklebreakers.
Ioana smells pungent spices from the curry stall.
She's hit with acetone fumes from the nail bar
in Takapuna Mall.
Teen dwellers, let off the leash for a day, hunt in packs.
Mini shorts and puffer jackets for survival.

She overhears debates.

They protest, but what for?

News at six, delayed at seven but she isn't home until eleven.

She will set her alarm for six thirty.

Ioana will eat nutella for breakfast, and this is her history.

Selina Tusitala Marsh

Girl from Tuvalu

girl sits on porch
back of house
feet kicking
salt water skimming
like her nation
running fast
nowhere to go
held up by
Kyoto Protocol
An Inconvenient Truth

this week her name is Siligia
next week her name will be
Girl from Tuvalu: Environmental Refugee
her face is 10,000
her land is 10 square miles
she is a dot
below someone's accidental finger
pointing westwards

the bare-chested boys
bravado in sea spray
running on tar-seal
they are cars
they are bikes
they are fish out of water
moana waves a hand
swallows
a yellow median strip

moana laps at pole houses
in spring tide
gulping lost piglets
and flapping washing
girl sits on porch
kicking

Dinner with the King
For Tui Ātua Tupua Tamasese Tupuola Ta'isi Efi

Crab soup broth
Coriander, lemon grass,
Clear as the conversation between us
You ask
What's happening with our people in New Zealand?

Oka is announced
In a crystalline voice
From you, the choice of my people
Cool sliced cubes of fish
Flesh speckled with salt, lemon juice
Swim in onions, a splash of coconut cream
Raw as Nelson's hunger for Independence
As bitter lemon sweet as Tamasese's peaceful
Call for freedom
At Tuaefu
We marinate in history's juices.

Mains come
Sunset slab of salmon
An upturned cup of rice topped with curry
Green salad laced with peelings of papaya
You speak of desire for balance
Mau Samoa whose fierce independence
Is priceless
You place small grains of rice on my plate
What's happening with our people in New Zealand?

I speak of the rising generation of gafatele
Those of many bloods
The urban resurrection of spoken

Word and song
Chanting over the many places they belong
Rooted in Aotearoa.
I speak of e-books and twitterature
Self-publication, Facebook and literature
Of Al's Prime Ministerial Award
Of Lani's storming of Amazon.com
Another place where we belong
Gathering kindle, setting fire with words
Setting fire to worlds.

Vanilla bean ice-cream atolls
Rise from a sea of mango and pink guava
Tickling our throats
You speak of horizon-seeking
And of ways before papalagi, sky breakers
Met us, earth dwellers
We watch Tusi Tamasese's
O le Tulafale, a Samoan pacing
Lush silence, verdant Va
The space between us beautified.

Pinot noir and coffee
We drink in Seamus Heaney
Inhale Il Divo and Viktor Frankl's
Search for Meaning
Afters before us.

Entering Pouliuli
For PBMM

Gender is too shallow
a pool

for our gods
to dip a toe

or lick their shimmering
visage, but I've always thought

Pouliuli to have
more male

than female
energies, and I know

he's not strictly
a god, like

you've never heard
the one about how

Pouliuli ensnared the Rā, the sun
or crushed Māui

between his toothed walls
but as you and I

contemplate entering
Pouliuli, I see us

male and female Māui
crawling into death

seeking truths of deep
mysteries, followed by

pīwakawaka's laughter
and history begins.

Ria Masae

Vinyl Sundays A-Track

We genuflect.
Men dressed by their wives in their Sunday best
kneel on planks of uncross.
Women pass over bread
to their children to deposit in pass-around plates
for confessional clean slate.

Samoan choir sing praises to Jewish mythology.
Tagaloa spits an eye for an eye at our irreverence.
He laughs, foreseeing
my first taste of alcoholic lust
is sipping the blood of Keriso.

Mā

You look at me plastic
 'Why don't you have a malu?'

 Pfft:
the memories of my ancestors
and stories of their villages
are not tattooed on my skin
because I am no kin
to pālagi parlour needles
nor do I feel I have earned the tap-tap-tap
of the sausau mallet on the au
— the fine-tooth comb of bone —
held in the sacred lima of a tufuga.

I have no desire for my body
to advertise pepelo
to billboard bullkaka
to grandstand airs
for show
for fashion
for Likes.
I have no need for my tino
to house my mana
in a sham temple
like you.

Gripping sand

My feet sink into the sand
as I tramp across the tanned shores
of my grandmother's village in Samoa.
Waves do not rush in to greet me
I have been away too long and
this slice of the Pacific Ocean
does not easily forget.

I stop and look out into the sea
pristine as the travel brochures portray
      no need for Photoshop
      no government development plans
      no colonisation

I close my eyes and wait . . .

The messenger wind breezes
salty words into my ears —
      You may have taken your first breath
      on the fanua of my kin, Aotearoa
      but you have neglected the umbilicus sands and waters
      where the kenese of your
      existence is rooted.
The cool breeze leaves me then
to be beaten by the sun's rays.

I did not notice I was gripping the sand
until I felt silk granules spill from
the Va between my toes;
grains of late yearning
slipping into a lost past.

Courtney Sina Meredith

The internet told me to go for a run

The internet told me to go for a run
I walked to the park with good posture
The sky asked me to catch it while it fell
I opened my arms to their maximum
The house said it needed a vacuum
I loaded the dishwasher and turned it on
The silence wanted its throat slit
I sang to myself while I made dinner

How about being a woman?

How about being a woman?
How about being a young woman?
How about being a young brown woman?
How about being a young brown queer woman?
How about being a young brown queer single woman?
How about being a young brown queer single educated woman?
How about being a young brown queer single educated professional woman?
How about being a young brown queer single educated professional creative woman?
How about being a young brown queer single educated professional woman?
How about being a young brown queer single educated woman?
How about being a young brown queer single woman?
How about being a young brown queer woman?
How about being a young brown woman?
How about being a young woman?
How about being a woman?

Brown girls in bright red lipstick

Brown girls in bright red lipstick
have you seen them
with their nice white boyfriends
paisley scarves on scarred shoulders
looking for their wings

Brown girls in bright red lipstick
where the hell are they it's Sunday
driving 80s commodores
knees dangling kitchen benches

Brown girls in bright red lipstick
have you seen them
with their nice white girlfriends
reading Pablo Neruda
on fire the crotch of suburbia

What's inside her
fingers Jesus penis
the old testament
she's promised to a Tongan welder
or a buff Cookie cliff diver

Brown girls in bright red lipstick
have you seen them at the beaches
drowned in virgin olive oil
twirling their hair into soil

Brown girls in bright red lipstick
rearranged up on the stage
making your soft brothers
run broken home to mother

have you seen them washed in twilight
struck by hours and the colours
running like mascara
taking yet another lover
she can't sleep she's walking thunder

Brown girls in bright red lipstick
have you seen them in the kitchen
shucking mussels cutting chicken
egging on the lone horizon

her dark centipedes are hidden
Manu Sina's glittered lace
are they veins or blue pathways
led to reddest change.

Kim Meredith

Dance of Sina

you are a tiny flutter
a marigold on the water
flung out calling the dead.
You are the Tui
across four winds,
an armour of feathers
of bone and light,
soaring over mountains
climbing the day.
You are the core
spilling seeds.
You are deepest blue
head first into soul.
You are blood
woven into silk
piercing night to sun.
You are a child
a child,
lost at sea,
anchored
on your mother's lips.
A young girl
broken into woman,
jagged coral
holding the shore,
fingers caressing
Tamaki river
unfolding on the Waitemata,
you are the song
from your ancestors
sung into being.

Love Letters from Glen Innes

I

I saw my father, he'd missed the last step getting off
the bus. An elderly woman helped him to his feet
led him safely over the road, his right eye swollen like
an aubergine. He said over and over it happened so fast.

II

Past brooding horses, flanked by blackberry bushes
these magnificent bodies up close unnerving.
I'd watch them on weekends, lean against the wooden
railings, trying to work out how they slept standing up.

III

I planned my escape sitting at the bus stop, strange faces
peering out from the Led Zeppelin T-shirt my mother gave me.
Friends fly past on pushbikes, shouting as though it's been ages, they
ride back with rolls of toilet paper tucked under their arms.

IV

You lean forward to catch my words, take your shoes off.
We start across the black storm pipe past the warning signs.
In the water below eels swim upstream unfurling. We arrive
on the other side to your brick house where you grow quiet.

V

You're wearing the Bruce Lee T-shirt. Your poppa calling
don't be late for dinner. We head down the shortcut on the way
to my place. You remember it was your nan who found my father
on the footpath. She told you over and over it happened so fast.

Karlo Mila

Touch in the age of COVID

I am walking,
recording
poetry on my phone,
for the first time.
The sound of my own voice,
making
verse
out-loud.

Words enter
the sounds of silence,
on a city playlist
that's never been so hushed.
An inner city playlist
I've never heard before.

There is something
about the very ordinary man
doing squats in the park
that makes me want to run to him:
tackle him,
bowl him over,
jump on him,
kiss him on the lips.

There is something
about the ordinary dad
with the bike helmet on,
ushering his kids safely
on the bridge
within a two-metre radius.

He is suddenly
all-the-kindness
and it makes me
want to put my hands
gently, on the sides of his helmet,
and say, hey,
I love you.

There is something
about the lone wolf man
on the horizon
in his noise cancelling earphones
standing on Mt Roskill
taking photos of the setting sun.
I want to say, hey,
Let's meet under
the next full moon?

There is something
about the guy running
in his kung fu shoes
with his dreadlocks bobbing,
I want to say, hey,
Run home with me —
straight into my bed.

I want to say
to the two
impossibly athletic
tall blonde men,
speaking Russian
to each other,
in impossibly tight-bright tracksuits:
hey, wanna threesome?

It's like joining a dating app
in the time of COVID —
a dating app
when no one
can really date.

There is something
about the *untouchable*
that makes me
want to *touch*.

Tūhoe Boys

I said to my mate
I'm going to write an ode
to Tūhoe boys,

She said, Don't.

But I've never been good
at doing what I'm told

I think maybe
Tūhoe are the Tongans
of Aotearoa.

The way the Ngāti Porou
are the Samoans,
Te Arawa are the Cookies,
and Ngāpuhi are the Niueans.

I get myself in trouble
for saying racist things like this.

But it would explain my attraction.

A Tūhoe boy I once knew
said that instead of
flash oratory
on the marae
he set the bait traps
in the forest.

That was his ritual,
I was impressed.

Even though I love me
a good whaikōrero.

A Tūhoe boy I once knew
said after the revolution
and there was no tino rangatiratanga
everywhere
he wanted to know,
what we would eat for breakfast.

Then he set about decolonising
his diet, bypassing the supermarket
getting his milk
directly from a cow
growing his own green
making his own cheese

walking the talk
cooking the cook
eating the eat.
I thought maybe
he was the man for me.
But he didn't agree.

That's ok.
Because you can lead a horse
to water,
but if you can force them to drink
they aren't a Tūhoe boy.

Maybe I like them
cos they tend to be short
but they can fill up a room
with jokes, and story, and ihi and wehi,

in the way that they become a mountain
and every other man
stands
in their shadow.

This would be too much
If they weren't schooled
in the fine art
of self-deprecation

I like this in a man.

A Tūhoe boy I once knew
in his mid-sixties,
once blew off facilitating a panel
at a conference,
because he wanted to keep on
talking to me.

I like my men like that.
A bit rogue.
Kind of rude.
Fucking charming.

A Tūhoe boy I once knew
was all nervous shimmer in a room.
Whenever you looked at him
he wasn't looking,
I knew he was watching.
Everything.
I could feel it,
and he could feel it back.

You gotta be careful of those ones.
They'll catch your interest
with a story not meant for you
but meant for you,
a buck each way.

I'm a sucker
for a gambling man
who can carefully
calculate the odds
otherwise known
as cheating.

I'm the daughter of one.
Maybe my dad
is the most Tūhoe Tongan
you could ever meet.

I once knew a Tūhoe boy
who said poetry was his job.
He called waiata song-poetry
and haka dance-poetry.

Then quoted some Pākehā academic
pretended he couldn't remember
her name
and couldn't pronounce it.
He asked for help.
Her name fell off my lips.
That cunning dumb,
in the name of trying to catch
how clever you are.

They don't give a shit
about first impressions
it's all about them sussing
whether you are a dick or not.

Us Tongans do that too.
It's called fie-vale-loi,
this translates
'wanting to be stupid: lying'.

I know that game.

Bluster, bluff, buffoon
all in the name of
I don't give a shit
but, actually I do.

I once knew a Tūhoe boy
who could see dead people.
I find that kind of thing attractive.

Which may be why I'm still single.

One day
I might meet a short mountain
named after a tupuna
who can tell good jokes
write dance-poems and song-poems
wring the necks
of his own free-range chickens
feed me sweet, happy eggs on toast
and make a self-composting toilet
to protect the mauri of his ancestor
the river.

I might
make him mine
for a moment
before he returns
to the mist.

Maybe.

After Reading Ancestry
For Albert Wendt

Page by page,

I found myself dreaming, paddling feet
in the lush green grass of Mānoa, Hawaiʻi
sand under surveillance at Long Bay,
at the table of Palagi breakfasts in Samoa,
circling an unfamiliar umu pit.

But all roads lead to Ponsonby
where restored villas ascend,
skylighted, into lagituaiva,
and the leaves still speak
the gentle green-tongued talk
of tended gardens.

You, Albert,
character among your characters
appear, a dreaming woman
at your side, flourishing.
The soil of stories in your hands

You kneel together,
planting the strangers of our sleeping lives.
Past and present collide
in one single kernel,
unfolding beyond the boundaries
of dream. Taking their own shape,
orbiting out into a garden

of pūkeko, people, aloe vera, eels
light, lettuce, mokopuna
named fine mats,
feijoas, family gods, fungus
and freedom trees.

We are all permanent guests
of landscapes you've created.
The nuances of red
bloom. The caramel generation grow,
practised schizophrenics, surviving
the small humiliations of raw peripheries.

You've traversed it all,
charting outsider territory
with black star
after black star,
before us.
The relief of
another way of mapping.

Death will come
and still your garden will grow,
owls circling softly overhead.

Once you've imagined it possible
to gafa back to Atua,
the story can never be the same again.

Sakaraia Nasau

I Miss You

I miss,
The feel of running my hands in water,
the water spraying on my face and clothes,
washing my face and 'salty eyes' in Dilo water so I can sleep at night

I miss,
jumping off the boat to help others pull it on to the stone,
jumping from the tree vines to cool in the crisp water at Daku,
swimming at Mataisuva where big crashing waves throw us ashore.

I miss,
going to the teitei to pick sweet bu juicy watermelon and mangoes,
the salivating mana with creamy miti fresh ota and sticky uro-ni-vonu,
Bu Duli's rich moist, brown-sugar pudding — almost like chocolate cake

I miss,
visiting you in Vutia
your grave covered with traditional tapa,
colourful flowers from the village brightening your space,
listening to Taitai and Bu tell stories about you.

They say I'm like you —
— my smile
— my happy persona
— my gestures and posture
— and my love for the village.

A boat ride across the open sea to Vutia is the only way I can
visit you now.

I miss you, Papa!

Richard Pamatatau
Language

Some people say if you don't speak a Pacific
Language like your mother or father
then you are a plastic Islander.
Blastic saying p as b eye lander.

But Auntie Ena always said, in her St Heliers' home,
make sure you pronunciation your words prop lee,
and can you pass me a peijoa
and put it on a blate.

In Samoa at the surf camp
where tourists sleep in fah lays, the
hostess said come and get a fruits
with your coffees.

In Rarotonga the tourists gather at LBV,
Le Bon Vivant.
French style bastries and donuts.
TripAdvisor gives 4 from 5.

Just like being in Paris,
without the French and the traffic
and the crowds.
But not like Ponsonby Road.

Because when you are not a
plastic islander and there for a break,
what you want is a koffee.
Just like in Aukilani where the

Islanders have flown.
Fresh off the blane to
pronunciation their words properly
so they can peel a feijoa for a plate.

Cuisine rules

If you don't mind me saying you look like a savage,
the Australian lady said at the Wellington dinner party.
Are you by any chance a person who is ethnic,
said the marketing woman for tinned corn-beef.
Does She Know What An E C G Is asked the red-haired doctor,
when speaking about my mother, who ran a hospital, at the outpatients' clinic.

How the red-haired doctor treats an Island woman at the clinic,
could be construed as culturally savage.
At medical school they try to teach them a doctor
needs great people skills, like the host of a party,
if they don't want unhappy clients with a beef,
based on treatment that framed them as ethnic

Another day another night market, just what you want from ethnic
communities who are often too fearful to present at a clinic.
They sure know how to use spices with beef,
because cooking and colour is where they are not seen as savage.
We welcome them to the party,
the same way at a car crash we welcome a doctor

Did you say you are a doctor?
Gosh, you have done well for a person who is ethnic.
Your English is good, you'll fit in at the party,
which is in some ways a bit like a society's clinic;
At times savage.
Not really the place for a beef.

Have you tried the beef?
It's very good, just what the doctor
ordered when your hunger is savage.

It's been made with skill, by an ethnic
person, who is a doctor and works in a clinic
who recently joined a political party.

Isn't this the most divine room for a party?
The designers won't have a beef,
It's fun and chic not a medical clinic.
Our mix of guests includes a doctor,
who, as we like to mix it up, is ethnic
but not the least bit savage.

There are times when savage thoughts emerge at a party.
And ethnic people have a legitimate beef,
especially when working as a doctor at a clinic

Mele Peaua

My journey

I'm a cleaner. That's who I am.
It's about my family.
I clean for my children and my grandchildren
so they will be well-educated
and have a better life.
But also I'm a fighter.
I fight for my brothers and sisters who are cleaners.
I fight for the living wage, for the fair pay agreement.
I work hard for myself
but I fight for the collective.

When people say 'cleaner' they mean little people.
When they ask your job,
if you say a doctor, they say, 'Hello',
if you say a cleaner, they say, 'Hm'.
I fight for that respect. We need respect.
They have to remember that without the cleaner
their business can't open.

If you fight for the cleaner,
take the heart of the cleaner with you,
love the people you work for
then they know and trust you.
I'm a cleaner. When I speak to a cleaner
I will touch their heart
because they know I've been there.
Always remember where you've been
because that's the light that keeps you going.

Who is listening to this fight?
The cleaners are listening, because they work long hours

just to get enough for living.
They don't have enough time for their families.
The labour workers are listening
because they get the minimum wage.
Half of New Zealand is listening
because they are on low wages.
But our story will be the story of the living wage.
Another story will be of how grateful we are,
because the living wage will be the best
for the whole of New Zealand.

We came from the Islands
looking for a better home.
But it's not magic, the better way of life.
You have to fight for it.
You set up a goal. You're in the darkness
but you see a bit of light coming up.
You follow it and you get to the end.

Many Pacific people are cleaners.
We do it because New Zealanders don't want to.
But us, we never say no, we have to.
If you don't work, there's no food on the table.

Our people have the lowest education.
If you come from a background of low income,
you have that strong will to change it.
I learnt to speak on behalf of the cleaners
— What do we want? The living wage.
— When do we want it? Now.
That's the message we have to deliver.
We have a heart of fighting, and we never give up.

Niavā Pili-Tavita

My mother is like no other

She got involved in a fight in the village
Someone got hurt
Too badly, she needed to go to the police
The police comes looking for Mother
He finds a woman doing her washing at the
tap
And asks: 'I'm looking for Serafina'
To which she replies:
'Oh you just missed her. She left to go to
Apia.'

A week has passed by
And another policeman turns up
Mother saw him from afar
Turning, walking straight towards her house
Mother quickly goes to the toilet
And tells Father
'If he asks for me
Tell him I had gone to Apia to get some
shopping.'

Another week has passed
And the policeman comes back again
Mother saw him from afar
Then quickly climbs the 'ulu tree
And stayed up there
Forever.

My mother is like no other.

My mother makes the best koko Samoa in our
street

She happily shares a cup or two
With anyone else who walks past our fale
So, there was this guy
Our neighbour
He loves Mother's koko
so much . . .
He got addicted to it
And would buy Mother a bag of sugar every
other week
On his pay day
So that Mother could continue to make more
koko Samoa
For everyone who walks past our fale.

My mother is like no other.

My mother would never run out of money
As she banks it all in the corner of her ie
lavalava
in a tie
Even when my dad thinks there is nothing to
eat
With the fa'alifu fa'i for dinner
My mother would then untie the knot
And calls one of us
To run to the village shop
And get two elegi (tinned fish)
For dinner

Even when she won the lotto
Of seven thousand dollars and a bit
She refused to take her money to the bank
So, she tied it to her ie lavalava
And carried it with her all day long

Even when she had to climb
The 'ulu tree

My mother is like no other.

My mother is our bank
Where my Tongan brother would ask for a 'do
hundred dollars' to borrow
Where my ma'i brother gets a twenty to fill his
petrol
Where my island brother gets much support
through a phone call
And on one particular day my mother reveals
She pays for my nieces' school fees
And I might add, and materials too
Like her smart phone and brand new laptop to
name a few

My mother is my bank too
Where I send my daughter for a pasese to
catch the bus to school
But one morning she refused to go ask
She was mā (embarrassed)
That I had to ask my mother for money every
other week
Yeah . . . that year in particular, I just couldn't
make ends meet

My mother is like no other

Anyways, my mother is my bank
Where I exchange my Australian dollars
With New Zealand ones now
Whenever I visit her

She loves to add to her collection
And uses them only when she goes to the
island
Not for a holiday!
Most probably the next family fa'alavelave

My mother is like no other.

Doug Poole
Tuailemafua

I
Henry owned the
Fish & Chip shop
On Henderson Valley Road
He caught his own fish
He smoked his own mussels
The Henry Burger was world famous
In west Auckland

Henry lent his brother
His fishing boat
and nets
His brother lost it
Henry forgave Peter
Found it moored
in the harbour

Henry took his younger
brother David fishing
on the Manukau
A shark pulled them along
The water a raging storm
Henry jumped into the water
And cut the shark free

Henry was deployed
during the Malayan Emergency
a secret he whispered
told us to never tell; War is hell
people go missing

Henry came home
His brother Paul
wore his uniform
Told the girls he was
An American G.I
Paul is such a dreamer
He is the eldest

Henry part-owned
a racehorse just
like his grandfather
Henry won on horses
Henry was called The God Father
at the TAB
Henry would give you the shirt off his back

Henry stayed home
From the funeral
when his brother
John died.
Henry was too upset
and too unwell
to drive to Ruakaka

II
Henry's father was
Henry Stowers
His mother was
Edwina Ulberg
His grandfather was
Henry Ulberg
His grandmother was
Tuaoloa Fuatai Tuailemafua
His great grandfather was

Posala Siasau Tuailemafua
His great grandmother was
Fiane Silotoa Fuimaono
His great great grandfather was
Si'uli Tuailemafua
His great great grandmother was
Gogosina Afitu Lavea

III
Henry cried retelling
Unbeknownst to him
his name was changed
to Henry Raymond Saveileo
his grandmother gave him
his title, along with his brothers
Paul, Johnny, and Peter

Henry is the second eldest

Henry is Tuailemafua

The light I had hoped

I

As a child I would lie awake listening to my grandmother slapping
clothes on her bedside chair, speaking aloud her thoughts of the day,
clicking rosary beads and whispering her prayers

She carried a burden: being the last one, alone with transgressions;
going against her father's will; losing her young husband. When Uti
and then Maria died she became darker, she slept longer

My incessant demands for her memories, she would say, *I'm tired,
I don't remember, it was a long time ago.* When I greeted her in
Samoan, *'Talofa, oa mai oe'*, even this did not bring the light I had hoped

II

Your right index finger was caught in the wringer. Fists clenched as
you hung onto life, awaiting your grandchild's birth

Your hand would smack my hand, Christ's eyes in the lounge room
would follow my sins

Holding your hands in the dark toilet of Apia hospital. Your hands
patting me to sleep with stories of our Aiga

*The Patched hole in the homestead roof, your Grandfather's 1899 reminder
Sina feeding the gogo birds at night, her hands sweet*

I think of your arthritic hands in pain. Our hands — letting go —
falling — waiting to be held again

III

Planting Hawaiian hibiscus and radican gardenia, Sister Edwina
was right we were going to plant a hibiscus in the middle of your
garden. We planted mistakenly gardenia

It's where she wanted it, is supposed to be there, leave it

Hibiscus trumpet blooms waiting old stories true, some
superstition, some dream weaving too, of the old people, Upolu,
Tulaʻele our village. We know you have gone home

at sunset you run from tree to tree
the breadfruit, mango, paw-paw of
your mother's garden, stealing fruit

John Pule

I try to leave with the sun

where did that small juvenescent path lead to/ unnecessarily spill my
mother's blood when I was born/ several birds found a way into my
mouth/ one decided my tongue generated enough heat to make her
nest/ the other went further looking for solace in my mother's voice/
my feet a kind of indigenous plant uprooted from saint elsewhere/ last
night a sleeping child inspired the moon in the river to behave like a
foetus/ ants taught my mother invisibility/ that tree is taking its time to
kiss god/ is this the tree my mother planted the day I was born falling/
is the sun that warmed it over the years losing interest/is the wind for
over 60 years singing of dreams/hopes & desires found another sapling
to sing to/ these past days I struggle to live/exhausted/tribulations/tired
of the anxieties/the storm in my soul/the shark I was born with/aging/
unable to sleep/my grandmother's name atahelagi means a clear view
of the after world/ she saw the bird leave my mouth/she saw I would
develop wings later when I was new/ when words could not describe the
meaning of clouds/ that rose triumphantly in the eyes/ that succumbed
to the first time I spilt sperm/ like the white shorts I wore at baptism/and
the fragrance of my urine stung my senses/ I try to leave with the sun/ I
struggle to make ancestral hair from pews/ oh the miracle of windows/
the miracle of doors/ at the door step of the lowest sky/ what must I give
of myself from my body to live longer/ the gods laugh/birds that pecked
at the protein in my poetry laugh/ even my ancestors laughed/ when
that bird left my mouth at birth it shat on my lips/in the morning/the
sun in my hair/ I tasted the goodbyes/ I dipped my hands into the shit/
and after 60 years I saw remnants of paradise/or a land that resembled
my mother's eyes/like my brothers we miss her/there really is no turning
the soil that tasted blood at my birth into a warm blanket/ that one star
that shone in the night/ that is enough/ that one shadow of the priest
who blessed me is enough/ and when that time rejuvenates the fire you
lit the day you woke up/ remember this/ when we arrived to Aotearoa/
we had left behind our placentas/on an island in the middle of the

Moana/ my sleep is a stone my sky is a bit of blood my night is a paper
so I say to you all I offer is a bird that melts into a shape of passport
and because I cannot move to the sea I am a tree who can see my fruits
if the sea cannot see me/that sad horizon is my eternity/that owl has
eyes full of vases/that ship is the colour of my journey/roads that end in
newspaper and stones/now that I know who you are/I want to rest awhile
to understand your silence in relation to the radio's piousness/a door
that waits for you/that room is the moon's harbour/that window has
closed its world/ I wait for the bus's poetry/I wipe away the salt from the
pillows jaw/to see a landscape's jubilance /for now I cannot leave until
the sun leaves/you stay I go

from 100 love poems (1995)

to end my voice with time, space and sea/ to stand up because the world has a place for me/ to leave behind my songs, hopes and desires/ because I had no more room in my dreams for them/ after lifting my hands out of sun and light-time/ I stand on the shore faced towards the north/ recite my genealogy/ tie my names to the air/ watch wings develop as night falls once/ recite a poem that is the most luminous/ lift my feet out of water and moon-time/ for the last time see my face is really blue particles/ for the first time see a ship leave without a map/ I sit down and sands slip away as I begin one last attempt to return to your house in the sun

Looking at rain too long has given me eternity

Looking at rain too long has given me eternity.
A mirror cut away my country and sea.
I lived in a fruit that fell from a child's hand,
now I cry when the moon is in my dream.

I was made out of wood and my heart
was full of saltwater; chasing a shadow from
my body led me to this secluded room,
here I watched the horizon be a photograph,

I fled to another part of the land.
My stomach was shaped like a sack of apples.
I left behind the seeds to ignite some joy.

One day you will wake up from all this dreaming,
that all there is really to see and know
eternity is a mirror for our children.

Nafanua Purcell Kersel

Modesty Tasi, Lua, Tolu

Tasi. Skinny Dip
they take your hand they pull you to sea they stop.
— why bother with clothes?
— those people are miles down the beach — only dogs and gulls can see
[that]
their pale skin is free
and yours is not.

Lua. That No One is Watching is never true
because the fish
the molluscs the seaweed the sami

carry your nakedness in their shimmer and guts,
shell and sucking cups
through green brown blue-black waters

give you over to
the backs of turtles, stingrays and whales
passing Goddesses, Gods in underworld gaps
to lap up onto your family's beach

ten thousand holograms of you naked
will wash up in foam
at FalealupoatSatufiaatAleipata to be
stomped on
by white-clad aunties
and behatted mamas
because of course, it's Sunday.

and they'll cut your hair
take you to church

and throw you at the floor
to be prayed upon

they might even
send your image packing
down into Pulotu
summon the serpent aitu to come and feast
tau-sami on your flesh.

Or, a palagi man may find you
with his red swollen face and raw disease in his folds
settle his bright eyes on you
and shame you
out of your skin

        [he might slap his skin
onto yours]
and say, you don't know any better
and say, you should not have tempted
and say, you are his now anyway
so you cover up.

        [how his ancestors
taught yours?]

because if creatures recognise your
flab   crevice
  malu   coarse hair

they get to claw
your goodness
right out of your being
and spit it back into the sea.

That no one is watching is never true.

Tolu. Lavalava Lost

you dive deep   [into your element]
greet Atua   [wet kindred]
who wash   [off the white ash]
and watch you
swim   [your freedom]
beyond your skin.

Face Recognition

The it's ok I'm used to it face/you can stuff your
job face/
no, you go first face/
The Resting Brown Bitch Face//

God-fear Sunday face/
typeset/typecast face/
The Placeholder Diversity Face/solemn lies on Fridays face//

The Side-eye Squad Face/white space/down face/
Les Mills trained face/start us with a song face//

The Sidekick Sista Face/brown card carrying face/
you think you're smart face/smart is not enough face/The Bruised Face//
The Gauguin Face/Disney face/Porn Hub search face/
crunk face/selfie face/make a tea for Aunty face//
The dusky face/rape face/
you know better face/
gossip face/gone native face/
we've been here before face//

the fight face/the brown face/
the shame face/the brown face/
the crime face/the brown face/
the drug face/the brown face/
the gang face/the brown face/

The FUCK YOU Face/the brown face/

the brown face/
the brown face/
the brown face/

the brown/face/
the brown/
face/the brown/
face the brown/

face the brown/Face//

Melanie Rands

Banana Poem

when he brought them home from the cossie club
she didn't want to know
but he planted them anyway
some bananas and a row of taro

o'e u'u o'e u'u

when he planted taro and bananas
she was secretly hoping they'd die
but before she knew it
they were ten feet tall
and starting to multiply

o'e u'u o'e u'u

they took in the volcanic soil
took the state house
bikes in the backyard
church on Sundays
folding chairs and the above-ground para pool
the holden in the driveway
beers and sausages on the
charcoal barbeque
they took the lounge suite
the kitchen table
the school
the murderhouse
and the mountain too

when he planted taro and bananas
she was secretly hoping they'd die

but before she knew it
they were ten feet tall
and starting to multiply

o'e u'u o'e u'u

soon word was spreading all over town
she hid from nosey neighbours
she thought, 'we're never gonna live this down'
and she waited until he was at work one day
and cut them right down to the ground.

when the boat comes down

when the boat comes down
a dadakulaci lies unconscious on the ground
4 nights of singing the horizon away
the banana boat swinging
16 knots into diesel sunsets
on her twin Armstrong-Sulzer 6 cylinder engines
Bob 'Gin' rocking her golden whiskey cabin
for 3 days straight
the night my father came
with 2000 tonnes of ripening cargo
her quota of islanders bursting
to over

f

l

o

w

kai vulagi on the bunks & everyone else down below and
all their spirits rolled into one
the night my father came
with whales' teeth and a turtle shell
on the Matua
all 355.2 feet of her round
Cape Brett
and up the Rangitoto channel
when the boat comes down
to Mrs Harvey's boarding house
on Hepburn Street in Freemans Bay
a gas stove and a double bed
in her refrigerated hold

Rosanna Raymond

Pulotu Pollution

Part 2: Some Old Flow
Grey day, wind is heavy, filled with the dead and the very much alive,
makes for noisy days out . . . no wonder nobody will look you in the eyes

London, Intentions, Tensions, Attentions

Everybody uploading tones of Babel

Chitter, chatter . . . Burble, babble, it all scrambles. Looks like the
matrix . . . pure maths, shame I am not good at numbers . . . but sure can
recognise a nuanced time inter-lapse pretext when I see one.

Personally I prefer somewhere quiet . . . . like the inside of a stone,
the sort that warm up when you hold them or put them in your pockets.

The old man Thames, got an old flow . . . somewhat aggro . . . he will take
lives if you let him, he's riddled with *taniwha,* I see them all the time,
heard they hitched a ride with the Dolphin . . . came in on a high tide.

'Who's that trip tropping over my bridge,' said the *Taniwha,* 'I'm going
to eat you up,' they laugh, it comes straight from the belly . . . so loud,
someone always calls noise control

Just go look under the bridges, they have even managed to chase the
odd troll away . . . making it a little harder to know who to pay and what
you're paying for

The shore is scattered with bones, I use them to make music so shrill, they
shake the gods from the trees . . . doesn't matter where they are from . . .
they come to hear that music, it has a familiar melody . . . they sing along

Circulating
Discharge
Relieved
Ejection
Reflected

In themselves, on the streets of London town

We walk side by side . . . hanging in the heavens with the lights on

Part 3: Polutu Pollution
Lights off and . . . just hit downtown *Lalolagi* . . . life under the clouds

On my way to *Pulotu* to catch up with the *tipuna,* some old friends and the gods.

Took me a while, the entrance is blocked with a global gathering of corporate sponsored rubbish, it's mainly plastic and ocean going.

The sound of money markets merges with the smell of fried chicken drowning out the *tangi* of the Blood Clot, sitting patiently at the doorway, with her legs crossed and a club in both hands, chewing *kava* . . . her *Malu* clinging to the posts of the house.

There's a flying fox nailed onto a stick . . . Jesus styles . . . or is that spread eagle, can't make up my mind . . . anyways . . . ever get the feeling you've been shafted

Desecration, Testament, Treatment, Excreta

No wonder the rocks and earth were weeping . . . or maybe they just been laughing too much

I had to go the back way through *Hawaiiki*

Hawaiiki Nui, Hawaiiki Roa, Hawaiiki Paomaomao

The Long White Cloud led the way . . .

Haere atu ra koutou kua wheturangitia hoki atu ki a Hinenui te po e,
Haere atu ra, haere atu ra, haere atu ra . . .

I follow the cry for the dead

The *Malofie* were there waiting to check me in . . . my passport to *Pulotu*
etched on my legs

I stop and talk with some old souls, they see I am a little anxious

They tell me 'don't worry babe, *Hinenui Te Po* has told all the necessary
bodies, the salt water whanau are coming from the all over the Moana,
they are weaving fine white mats and binding bundles of fuzzy limed hair.'

Blood Clot's *Malu* spies me and comes to speak to me.

I do as I am told, put my hands in the air, and drop my skin in one of
the puddles

The *tatatau* didn't go, it's deeply scored in my flesh, highlighting all the
spaces in between.

I gift her a bunch of red feathers, some necklaces I made for dancing
and praying and a couple of London based *taniwha,* one is half lion half
serpentine, the other a shapeshfiter, she is used to the muck and mirth
of mankind, she even copulates with them

They have brought a bottle of single malt scotch, some old magic charms
made out of red coral and acorns

All good ingredients for a soul shake down party, everybody turns inside out, dancing and praying, all at the same time . . .

Out come the guitars and the wood drums . . . gonna be one of those sing song . . . long nights . . . no room for wall flowers here . . . all the bodies get their tattooed arses on the dance floor

We sing songs of redemption and reciprocity

In comes the light, it shines so bright you can see into the corners of everybody's heart.

No secrets, no lies, the shadows take flight . . .

This is paradise baby, no heaven, no hell . . . I feel quite shiny . . . all warm and fuzzy and covered in the dust and the detritus of eons of past lives.

It's like a stain that never quite goes away

Well as you can imagine . . . I've lost all sense of time and space . . . and when I finally get back to *Lalolagi,* it's still dark . . . looks like I'm the last one back, so better go turn on the light.

Talk about the need to be switched on

Luti Richards

Papa

We did it
Reached zenith
Found Zion
Winked at the stars
And then each other
Entered joy unending
Because the mountain bowed — finally
The crushing waves actually gave way to us
Just as promised
Just as we hoped

Now watch me climb
Face in the rock
Spirit to the sky
Giving as you gave — perfectly
No longer waiting because it's here
Bound for those God-glory streets
Carving new roads
Building new cities
Stitching age-old reels
And writing brand new letters

Victor Rodger
Sole to Sole

Fahhhhh, man.
I'm
hungry.

> I'm straight up
> hangry.

Got any food?

> Sole, if I had any food
> it'd already be in my mouth.

Sad guy.
—

—

Gotta dollar?

> Nah, g.

I gotta dollar.

> Congratulations.

Egg.
If *you* gotta dollar
we could use *my* dollar
go get us a two-dollar scoop of chips at that place by the beach.

> Sole. I told you — I got *no* dollar.

Reckon if we ask
they'd give us half a scoop
for a dollar?

Like
if we ask really nicely.
Like
'Please, Sir.
We only gotta dollar.'

Pffffft.
Sole.
As *if*.
You've seen their scoops.
They're stingy as.

Yeah,
true.
Guts.

Yeah.

—

—

Fahhhhh, man.
Look at that afakasi kid though.
He's eating that Boston bun
like a lion
eating a deer
they just killed
on one of those nature shows.

Fahhhhh, man, he's always got food.

You see his nana at lunchtime?

        Nah?

Bro.
She brought him
K
F
C.

        To school?

Yeah, man.
Walked straight up to him
in the middle of the quad.
Gave him a three-piece quarter-pack, man.
Upsized.

        How do you know that?

Cause I asked him for some chips.

        Oooooh, shame.
        Did he give you any?

Like
one.

        One chip?

Yeah, bro.
One
chip.

Fahhhhh.
Sad guy.

Yeah, sad guy all right.
—

—

Hey!
Sssssssssssht.
Sole.
—

—

Sole?
Sssssssssssht?
Don't pretend you can't hear me
just cause you're wearing
AirBuds.
I know you can hear me.

                                                    What?

Gizza bite?

                                                    Of what?

Your bun.

                                                    But it's almost finished.

Yeah, we can see that.
That's why we wanna bite.
Before it's finished.

                                                    —

—

Come on, man.
Me and my uso here,
we're starving.

                                        So am I.

Bro.
You had KFC already.

                    I gave you some chips at lunchtime.
Seriously?
You gave me
one.
One
sad
stinky
chip.
But that was ages ago.
That's like
ancient history.
Like a mummy in a pyramid in ancient Egypt ancient history.
—

                              —

—

Go on, bro.
Please.
Gizza bite?

                                        —

—

Fahhhhh.
Fine.
Here.
Finish it.

You sure, bro?

You want it or what?

Oh, shot, bro.
You the man.
Yeah. You the man.

Anne Hollier Ruddy

Song of the Islands

We all stared up at her,
blinding white in the sun,
this foreign ship Mariposa
wrenching us from everyone.

The crowd sang 'Isa Lei',
we raised hankies to our eyes.
The sweet smell of frangipani
softened sad goodbyes.

Mum was sick in her bunk
the whole voyage long.
A steward held my childish hand
en route to the dining room.

Auckland at last, its wooden wharf,
buildings taller than I'd seen.
All were grey, water like squid,
I shivered — the wind was keen.

My father's face emerged
looking pale and stern.
Then understanding dawned —
a new life had begun.

Mum clutched her woven mats.
'You won't need those,' he said.
He gave them to someone else
as he walked on ahead.

Saulaina Sale

The Poet

Fisherman and wordsmith
active and passive, his line
is impeccable. Long or short, his drive

to the green is executed; so sweetly
that all the forces of nature
are cornered like iron filings

pointing to his ultimate destiny:
to organise and invent
new worlds of pure ecstasy.

Luaipouomalo Naomi Sauvao Pasene

'To Be a Samoan Woman'

Includes lyrics from 'Le Aute' by Ester Temusika

She sacrifices only for her downfall
to be the uplift of a whole village.
She *bows* with gracefulness,
she *dances* with gracefulness,
she softly composes her fingers
to trick the human eyes to believe she is a wave,
SHE'S A WHOLE STORM!
She is the result of tough love,
tough love disguised as 'To Be a Samoan Woman.'

Expectations,
are they biblical commandments?
or the *FA'ASAMOA* way?
and if by not abiding means
she is trespassing away
from her ancestors' dreams then,
how does she break free
from the chains of hierarchy?
Hierarchies of sex creates traditions,
traditions ruled by her village,
her village ruled by men.
Full of 'Tama'ita'i O Samoa'.
Samoan Woman who confused living as a chore,
and based their entire lives on four,
— words: graceful, obedient and *ata mai*!

In any given situation, she's graceful
as she sings —
'Le 'aute, Le 'aute, Le 'aute
Lo'u se'i, Lo'u se'i,
Manaia . . .'

She's as graceful as a flower,
but closeup she's tearful, eyes sour.
And still she dries them,
then serves her mothers that sit quietly and listen,
they teach her TO BE OBEDIENT!
FILEMU!
be quiet during the meetings you sit through,
and when told to move, move and apologise.
TULOU!
Not too low though, making sure not to trip up,
past the elders that discuss the family matters,
cause family matters, family will always matter.

And when they spoon feed her the word of God
she remembers they only want to save her from the pit of fire but,
who will save them? Who will save the AIGA?
Always in God's arms, but God was never the man that held a *FUE*.
Never the man that yelled 'DONT FORGET TO ATA MAI!'

Ata mai means to smile at me
let me see the stretch of the lipstick
smeared below your eyes.
She smiles and follows her hands,
E paia ou lima, her hands are sacred.
They're a mantelpiece for when her brothers go to war,
they carry the memories in frames, they bring *warmth* to the family.
Yet they grow cold from the empty warmth of womanhood

Samoan womanhood

Without lima o se Tina,
most villages would fall,
but she's tired of raising them.
she just hopes her *alofa,*

her *love* for samoan culture,
is not taken away or measured by the stain of sin,
cause to her, to be a Samoan Woman is just that,
to be samoan,
and to be fearfully,
A Woman.

'Talofa Mai Samoa . . .'

Dietrich John Soakai
Untitled

It's rainy season,
drunken songs echo through the night of my great grandfather's burial ground,
where he rests with the company of his brothers and sister,
His mothers and fathers.
We huddle under his Fale Samoa,
we MANLY hunters hope that our game over hears our cockiness

My mountain of an uncle in law talks of big game hunting
while my dad listens with a yeah right in one eye and a bloody Samoans in
the other

My father slurs under his drunk breath: Tuku ho Fia poto: Is a Tongan
phrase used to correct someone which means
'stop thinking you know it all'
or is used to rebuke someone who thinks their knowledge is more superior
than yours

In the Darkness photographs can't hold memories without a flash,
I guess that's why this island's thunder lights up the whole sky
The sky blinks again and illuminates my great grandfather sitting in the corner
cross legged, in his usual praying position,
like he was praying for his learned tradition of addiction to stop with us;
I look away in shame,
we take another shot in their memory

Guilt is a photo that I have tried to lose but seem to always find when
looking for light
While my mother land feels cold toward me as she dreams,
she often cries in her sleep around this time of the year

Acceptance from my mother's land is a bottle of Chinese rice vodka that
is never to be savoured,
but to be shot down
quickly
And just as quickly,
lightning falls from the sky and everyone can hear it hitting the ground.

Silence is a tin cup that is never meant to stay full
The sky blinks again and illuminates my great grandfather sitting in the
corner cross legged
in his usual praying position,
like he was praying for his tradition of alcoholic addiction to stop with us;
I look away in shame
we take another shot
in their memory

Eric Soakai

298 Urban Orators

My (over)confident kids,
My sometimes moipez
My all the time warrior scholars.

I call them boarder breakers
with enough mana to shake a room.
Tip it on its head the way all good
Indigenous scholarship does.

If you've heard them speak
you'd understand why
as Kaiako
we use metaphors of eating when teaching
and breathing when practising
Because in the Vā we tend to,
The consuming of knowledge is natural,
How quickly they learn is natural
like our Hyena laughs or reciting of tala
Long
Glorious
Natural.
They call themselves a bunch of mixed race hoodrats
Proudly they are the 298 Kurahood rats.

Even on a camp 5 hours
from Saute Aukilani
they are still Papakura to the bone
with little else on their mind to rep.

This reminds me what we have already known,
That space is transformational when alofa is present.

That knowledge, culture, wairua
can converge and connect whenua to fonua to vanua
when we see our students where they are
eye to eye.

Where they have much to learn
and much to teach,
as I have much to learn,
and much to teach.

You cannot tell me
the physical bodies we come into contact with
do not ignite and summon the ancestors within us
when we share breath, and space and time
Harmoniously and joyfully
Knowledge threaded between dry jokes and songs during class
This poem is for the streets
For the cul-de-sac that holds the same chaotic energy
You'd find out bush.
Where I work, we might not have the size or resource of other schools
But if nothing else we are the melted dolls who survived the fires of
colonial violence.
The children of Maui who weave together space
stand between realms like a bridge playing chicken.

These words are for my students
Who trusted me enough to take the chip from their shoulder
stack them on top of each other's
until we created a platform they could be seen and heard from.
I hope you are proud of your ngaue
the art you produce is inspiring.
Thank you for helping me
as I have helped you.

Forgive Yourself

Forgive yourself for the times you didn't know better
Forgive yourself for the times you did, and still did it.
Forgive yourself for the 'what if's' the 'maybes' and the prayers that were answered in a language you could not comprehend
Forgive yourself for the lack of comprehension, the poverty you were raised in.
Forgive yourself for being raised in poverty, this is not your shame to carry.
Forgive Papa and Langi for splitting.
Forgive yourself for not making it in time,
Forgive yourself for arriving too early,
Forgive yourself for wanting to be swept away with the waves,
Forgive yourself for the scars you hid under your clothes,
Forgive yourself for the negative talk
Forgive yourself for the back handed compliments
Forgive yourself for the broken families
Forgive yourself for the broken promises our families were built on.
Forgive yourself for not growing up to be your parents' standards
Forgive yourself for waking up with a different dream one day
Forgive yourself for not being God
Forgive yourself for being God
Forgive yourself 7 times, then 7 more times and turn your cheeks as you forgive until you're a ball of meat spinning
Spinning from the infinite momentum of love that comes when you finally free yourself from the things that stood in the way of forgiveness.

Forgive yourself and move on.

Zech Soakai

A Streetcar Named Diaspora

Poutasi silver,
red-and-rustic
melted plastic
and wheels with friction

the year was
two thousand and fifteen.

Cousin,

       Silafaga

thank you,
for this car,
this driver's seat,
this vehicle
— that zooms

melting present into future, kissing
future's cheek against the past's lips.

This car,
this thing
that race
we've won.

Your mana,
I have carried,
this car
 — that taonga

Second hand object of joy
I play, play, play
with this ta'avale
and remember:

What it's like to be home
here,
and there,
and what it's like to
race between islands
and know that I belong
to all of them.

Poutasi = village in Sāmoa that my mum's side of my family come from
Silafaga = the name of my Samoan cousin who gifted me his little metal
car to remember him by

Fesaitu Solomone

Fantabulous Blackie

A professional swimmer
Olympics here I come
Backstroke, front stroke, two stroke, no stroke
That's me in my element
No coach, no problem

They call me Blackie, I prefer Chocolate
Search and rescue, hola!
Hard to find, look closely
Camouflaged in golden black
Colourful as the rocks on the beach

They call me Sleepy Eyes, I prefer Popeye
That's my gift
Eyes closed, heart pumping
Glazed for target
On point as a killer bee

Hair curly and tangled, but not Rapunzel
Cuddly and fluffy, but not Winnie the Pooh
Chubby and round, but not Flubber
Cheeky and stubborn, but not Gargamel
I am figure eight not eighteen

I never give up
I never give in
I never bend down
I only look up for a crystal view of solitude
I am Blackie, fantabulous and splashing

Sala'ivao Lastman So'oula

Blackbird

They say
The truth is this
The truth is that
The truth is a lie
The actual fact is,

My people were never invited to this place,
We were hired, to replace,
Loose screws on machines that weren't up to scratch
The hired help,
A simple solution with invisible strings attached,
But we came anyway,
With hopes in our hearts and the sun on our backs,
They opened up the gates and we came flooding in on planes and ships,
They never understood our mother tongue and so we sealed our lips,
And silent we are still

We put on the boots with the steel tips,
And we walk, and we walk and we walk and we work,
In hopes the next generation can live for something better,
Wrapping our dreams in fluorescent vests only to be more invisible than ever,
Gotta make it, gotta make it, can't miss the next shift
Traded our way of life just for a quick buck,
Paycheque to paycheque that's how we live it up,
Wake up just to regret waking up,

But I gotta clock in,
And let the day begin,
Put the bag on the conveyor guide the mouth through the sealer,
Put the bag on the conveyor guide the mouth through the sealer,
I didn't get paid for the extra hours worked last week,

Put yourself on the conveyor guide your mouth through the sealer,
The temp worker doesn't get a say I guess,
I put myself on the conveyor now my mouth is through the sealer.
To become another product for the slave traders and dealers,
Coz I have seen this routine too many times before,
But it's been swept under pallets of the factory floors,
We stack and store and we stack and store,
Hopefully we don't get stacked and stored,
But when the boss asks, 'Overtime?'
And we reply, 'Sure'

We fill our lungs with tobacco smoke,
And breathe out pointless conversations,
'How was your weekend?'
'Got pretty waaaasted'
The type of questions on regular rotation,
About females,
About sports,
About work,
About females,
There's always that one guy who spins the best fairy tales,
He might talk alotta shit but that's entertainment for the day,
Because work is the same,
The same levers pulled,
The same machines working,
The same notches turned,
The same faces yawning,

The old timers try and school us during the break,
He sat there with a filter between his lips,
Spoke of disdain towards his job,
And with cigarette stained fingertips,
Pointed out the worst about people with power,
'It's bad enough that you get paid shit, but they treat you like shit too'

He says that's how capitalism works,
But we have families to support, our choices are limited,
Young man! Tone down your talk about equality,
You might get called a communist or a hippy, as if it were a bad thing,

The rasp in his voice spoke his truth,
I could see regret welling up in the corners of his eyes,
His longing for his Pacific trapped in his gaze,
Almost becoming a reflection of mine,
Were we destined to share the same ache in our spines,
The same blistered skin on our knuckles,
Is this the only pathway to provide?

I guess it's all part of the,
The production line
The production line
The production, lie

Onehou Strickland

Dusky warrior

On the shores of Narrowneck
I breathe deeply under a bucket hat
As an impromptu nap approaches

Recalling an archive of
the Maori Battalion,
1st and 2nd War of our one World.

Stood here, they did
learning a war cry to take across the ocean.
The newspaper called them 'dusky warriors'.

The dusk is my favourite time of the day.
The wind goes still, the sky turns fire.
I wonder if being dusky
means you stand
somewhere between the last sun
and the first star.

When my year 3 teacher asked us what culture we were,
We replied with Cook Island, Niuean, Samoan, Tongan.
She asked us if she could just call us all Maori for administrative ease.

They stood here, you know? Before sprinting into the ocean.
Forgetting for a moment what waits on the other side.
Dusky apparently also means shade or shadow.
I wonder if they were so big they cast silhouettes like mountains.

The apples on my tree at home are starting to fruit again.
Some will be darker than the others, some will join me on the beach.
Some will die before making it off the tree.

Being called Dusky started back with the painters
They painted us soft and supple, with full lips and dark red nipples.
Then more showed up to see the bare breasted maidens
and touch their cocoa brown skin.

The wind picks up finding a tunnel under my back
I tense my jaw, close my eyes and let out a sob.
No one knows,
No one can see
I am still under my bucket hat.

The Dusky warriors they called them.
I want to hold the name on my tongue
and not be confused by the taste.

I'd like to wear it like a badge, but it's covered in mud.
And bullets, and illness,
and hungry, unconsenting eyes.

The Dusky Maidens and Warriors watch on from the stars now.
As we remember what they went through, and wash it clean, just to
rewash it over and over.

Dusky is who I am.
For I am the dark red sky that welcomes the night.
The long cast shadow over the Earth. The still, red sky. The last bird song.
The Brown girl lying on the beach, that her Dusky tupuna once danced on.

Rev. Mua Strickson-Pua
Hip Hop Tag 2013

Bling bling
you aint got the money

bling bling
you aint got the honey

bling bling
you in the land of plenty

bling bling
you drowning in poverty

bling bling
you not laughing at comedy

bling bling
you knows it's called tragedy

bling bling
your wasting your time on irony

ching ching
you aint got the money . . .

Williamson Ave To Scanlan Street

15 to 28
Avenue to Street
Arrival to established
Fale to Whare
Aiga to Whanau
Beresford Street Primary to Mt Albert Grammar
Writing prize to published poet
Sunday school to graduate ordained Minister
Tautua to Mahi
Faith to Fa'atuatua
God to Atua
Scanlan Street runs off Williamson Avenue . . .

Faumuina Felolini Maria Tafuna'i

I am Sieni

I am Sieni
My mother is Sieni
My grandmother is Sieni
We were all born in the same house
We all swam in the same sea
We all grew taro in the same swamp
We all drank coconuts from the same plantation
We all stood on the same table when the king tides swept into our house
We all climbed onto the same roof when the sea waters flooded our home
We all waved goodbye from the same plane
when we were forced to leave our island
We all cried when we saw our house
in New Zealand
with neighbours we did not know
surrounded by a sea of concrete
and people who could not pronounce our name

I am Sieni
My mother is Sieni
My grandmother is Sieni
And this here, inside me, is my daughter Sieni
She will never know our little
house the warm embrace of
our sea
plant her own swamp taro
and rip the husk off coconuts from our
plantation
She will never be we
And we will never be she

Hulk for a Day

If I was a superhero for a day I would be
the Hulk
Is that bad that I want to smash things?

I'm coloured already — a nice cocoa brown
So I think apple green would suit me

As for the giant biceps — who doesn't want
those?
I'm Samoan too, so I already have Hulk
thighs

And it would be cool to also use Hulk lingo
'HULK ANGRY' 'HULK LEAVE' 'HULK HUNGRY'

Though I would try and be more poetic
'HULK PENSIVE' 'HULK PERPLEXED'
'HULK FAMISHED'

Maybe even multilingual Hulk
'HULK MALOSI' 'HULK TUMEKE' 'HULK
MAKONA'

And after a day of uncontrolled destruction
I would say 'HULK SORRY' 'HULK REGRETFUL'

Mere Taito
no frills

the mākutu potatoe sack
can fly you to Raiwaqa

cocoon you in a force field
so you can breathe through the clouds

lower you gently outside a bedroom window

you can step off
rattle the louvre blades
wake a family

breakfast with a favourite cousin
hear her say:
grace first please

say grace
wolf the long loaf slices thickly spread with Rewa butter
guzzle the sweet milky lemon leaf tea

tell her in between mouthfuls
how much she is missed

the mākutu potatoe sack
will fly you back to Hamilton

cocoon you in a force field
so you can breathe through the rain

lower itself gently outside the kitchen window

you can step on
shut the louvre blades
wave goodbye to a family

after you have asked:
thank you for the food, may I leave the table please?

tạn kạlu
For PJ

first words fall asleep
on the cave floor
of the mouth
when plosives
lose their aspirations

curling up beneath
the tongue
where it is warmest

or in between
the tight gaps of teeth

where light cannot
find them

they will uncurl themselves
long stretch into articulation
when the temamfua return
and gently massage
the mouth

open

the quickest way to trap a folktale

a research institution walks into a village
        scholarly clothes
        sharp alien tools
fine-spun birthmarks flow out of a magic twig
a wet metallic nose presses onto the thinnest
white flat bread that folds into a boat

a research institution gets to work
it asks us to open our mouths
we open
it lifts our tongues and prods
we sit very still
it pinches our uvulae with its forefinger and thumb
we do not gag
it pokes its head in and calls up to our nasal cavities
'hello, is anyone up there?'
'hello?'
we do not sneeze it out of our conscience
it holds a light into our eyes
we do not blink

a research institution collects its treasures
Mafi and Lu's marriage
annulled in a gazebo of hard covers
Raho's canoe
chopped and chiselled to stand like an antique spine
Moeatiktiki's congealed birth
moulded into an impractical jacket
Kirkirsasa's armpit tattoos
transfused into an overbearing gothic title
Tinrau's bird

taxidermised into a pretentious Preface
Puaknifo and Mostoto's fists
bloodied in Volume IX Footnote 8
Tiaftoto's oyster shell
shucked in a gloating Afterword

a research institution walks out of a village
      boards its white flat bread boat
      scholarly clothes
      the sharpest alien tool
      Copyright ©

Ruana Taito

Our faleoʻo

It looked like the other houses in the village —
all the families had their small beginnings.
There were boxes of clothes for all our big whanau.
My grandparents lay on their stomachs
reading their bibles.
There was the beautiful smell
of our neighbours cooking
fish, and taro with coconut cream.
My spot in the house was where my aunty and I
shared our sheet,
fighting over it as we pulled to win.
I always thought of my mum living in New Zealand,
how lucky she was to be sleeping on a bed.

Now, as I dreamed, I'm living in Aotearoa
and I want to go back with my whole aiga,
to do the things we used to do together
but our small humble faleoʻo is no longer there.

Elizabeth Talo

If I knew then what I know now / Poetic lemonade

A true product of perfection
At least that's what I'm meant to be
Crumbling from the inside out, I call for help
but the more I scream the more my voice floats
into the abyss
Silence
A true product of perfection
Shipwrecked. Abandoned.
As much as you say you love me, your love will
be the death of me I'm sure
A true product of perfection
Unrealistic Expectations
As I listen to the voices, my soul starts to disintegrate
Leaving me dry
A true product of perfection
Daydreaming of the good ol' days
When life didn't give one fuck about who you were
A true product of perfection
Before shade was thrown at you like rice on a wedding day
So carelessly done, effortlessly painful, tears
falling gushing down like it were Hunua Falls
A true product of perfection
If only someone had prepared me for the shit I
had learnt today but I guess when life throws you lemons
Fuck it, fuck you.
Fuck the lemonade.

Matafanua Tamatoa
Sunday Best

In her finest white dress, Mum parades around the sitting room
Dad, in his wheelchair, smiles and whispers his compliments
She smiles back knowingly, as this day is reserved for her best

Soon we will head out to church
We will listen to the hello's and how are you's of people we only tolerate on
Sundays before heading in
As always we reserve the seat behind the Pastor, his wife, their children and
God

A big white statue from Apia stands in the centre of the aisle
Beckoning us forward with his arms outstretched and sadness in his eyes
I stay back as my mum always said not to talk to strangers

People walk up and bow with respect and gratitude
I feel slightly out of place for I have none of each to give
Mum says we should do the same
So I follow and I stay silent as the others follow me,
like lambs in their white

I remain silent, fearful that I have nothing to say in protest
And if I did the stares of contempt would stain
And chaos would ensue
And I couldn't do that to my mum
For today is Sunday and she is dressed in her best.

Organics in Ōtara

Chairs from Mitre 10
Humbled by heavy bones
A greying mattress
Wet, with less foam
And less comfort to give
Simu's suit from five White Sundays ago.
Lint proud and unloved
Foreman's grill, blackened by the hassle of
Grilling for a family of six
Empty DVD cases, simmering in large boxes
Unwelcome and unlucky
As ripped pages from *Sweet Valley High* sway against the soft rain
The *Herald on Sunday* now soaked on a Tuesday
With big headlines of fading rugby players
And broke reality stars
Car tyres and a small bike from last month and last Christmas
All waiting patiently for the council to come.

Leilani Tamu

Researching Ali'i

I searched for you in boxes
    the archivist muttered *poison*

I searched for you in texts
    the librarian whispered *incest*

I searched for you in images
    the cashier demanded *money*

I found you in mele
    the people chant *aloha*

Aotearoa Runaway

they searched for my body
in local parks and schools

they cut away
the long grass
daring to hope
for a sign

an angelic proclamation
or at least a shoe or a sock

while on the other side of town
I was high in the sky
hanging out with some random guy

and my mate Johnny
in the backseat
last name: Walker
he was one real treat

then they found me
messed up and bruised
their sweet island girl
gone bush feral

forget sympathy (they said)
screw pity   yes to sheer relief
fuck yes to bloody angry

over and over they asked
and asked: what do we do

with this harlot, this slut?
what happened to our baby?

yesterday she was thirteen
years   innocent
now she's literally fucked

so they hacked off   my hair

hoping cultural violence: shame
might stop me from running again
but once more   I jumped
out that window   I hurtled

Nafanua hussy hair   flying free

far far away from Samoa
Aotearoa runaway
a foolish kid
searching

for true love
and freedom
from fear

Paradise Pasifika

Paradise Pasifika
Pasifika Paradise

our Pacific

they entered her and scoured her
for gold and silver
they named us and translated us
into their own way

of seeing the world

poly   mela   micro
nesian
many   black   little
island(er)s

in a Pacifique ocean

a passive maiden
ready for the taking
smothered in fake frangipani leis: hand-made in Taiwan
remembered in Tivaevae: woven in the Philippines

drunk on Jamaican rum and cockle shell beats

while making her money
from keeping Bad Billy's night club   afloat
living off European tourists
via gogo-cum-hula girls

desperate to stay in their Fijian bure

with their wet-dream island boys
as we remember the man
who named us
friendly   navigating   savages

the exploratory hero

who cut off chiefs' ears
in retribution for their sins
whose legacy lives on
in

the drunken   the toothless   the downtrodden

the ones who frequent the shadows
on street corners   licking their lips
laughing uncontrollably
as they siva
the memories of yesterday away

trying to forget

that these islands once belonged to their hearts
that this land once belonged to their ancestors
that this was once our
Paradise Pasifika

Pasifika Paradise

Mepa Taufa-Vuni

Feasting the eyes
(Talanoa with Frances Nelson)

I've watched them climbing the ladders of birthdays
I've watched them blowing their 1st and 21st candles
I've watched them getting poorer and poorer
'Why are your people like that?' others asked
They are feeding the eyes
Foolishly feasting the eyes of others

I've watched them giving away their *koloa*
Their fine mats and many more mats
Their toiled tapa thrown away for a *mafana*
I've watched them lining up at the loan sharks
I've watched them signing their life away
'Why are your people like that?' others asked
They are feeding the eyes
Foolishly feasting the eyes of others

I've watched them sleeping in garages
A tattered *tupenu* as curtains
Blocking out the wrenching wings of winter
I've watched their children huddling for warmth
Is this our 'mafana' — our warmth lost?
For foolishly feasting the eyes of others?
I've watched them forgetting their children
I've watched them ignoring education
I've watched them toiling for nothing
'Why are your people like that?' others asked

Others looked at them with sad sympathetic eyes
As they toiled in the land of milk and honey
Sweated and striven — working long hours with little pay

Just for foolishly feasting the eyes of others
Nothing for their children
Nothing for their future
Just feasting others' eyes
Just foolishly feasting others' eyes

Luisa-Tafu Tauri-Tei

Teine lelei

Listen
watch this Te Fiti turn to Te Ka
because I could speak in many tongues,
articulate to the moon, reverent soul in the way
that as I clench my teeth and exhale I say:
I am sick of making the ipu ki's for the guests.
Just me the obedient daughter.
Tulou. Tulou. Tulou.
In the corner of my eye sits my brother,
watching me bend my knees to show respect,
that little piece of . . . I straighten
the mismatched falas and wipe the portraits on the wall,
see my reflection in the glass,
how long must I wear this mask.
The mask of teine lelei: good.
Girl.

We have gotten so used to asking for forgiveness,
forgetting what apologies sound like when
they're not coming from our own mouths.
It seems like our bodies are conditioned for labour
from all the bridges we have built getting over our invisibility.
Getting over forgotten fa'afetai and fa'amolemole
men playing hide and go sleep
men playing hopscotch and bourbon and
the critics with their ratings like we're UberEats or something.
Or something.

Maybe our bodies are conditioned for labour
because our minds are conditioned to refill another's cup
whilst ours is constantly empty. Nobody remembers

to ask if we have had enough to eat or drink
and despite this I am weighed down.
My hands shake. And it's not because
of the 1321 cups of ipu ki I carry on my arms,
it's not because they're too heavy.
It's just I carry with me my tongue, my goldmine,
and learning to hold the heaviness of it has me tired.

Learning to hold it has me tired.
Learning to hold it has me tired.

But what about my mum?
And her mother?
Maybe these expectations have me sinking
into myself because I don't just carry my teine lelei.
I carry theirs. Their tatau of scars.
Rough hands that hold the same shape as mine,
yet hers feel too much like coal.

We have learnt to un shine.
Learnt to hide the gold we carry.
We have seen how the world treated West Papua.
We have seen what happens to goldmines in the Pacific.
Mum can I?
NO
Nan can I?
NO

Our mothers have tried to protect the treasures
wedged between our teeth
so that they aren't stolen out of our mouths
for they know all too well how willing
the world is to take.

How willing they are to take our mothers' teine lelei
and turn them into teine matuas.
We have been warned with every limping step
the effort it takes to lead a generation
when your backs have been used as stepping stones.
And so we are taught, to tulou, to smile,
to correctly guess how many sugars you want in your ipu ki
and so we offer up our backs for you to stand on,
only to uncrack our spine
retrain our minds
to lead
the next generation.

Because we have never been expected
to be teine lelei.
We have never been expected
to be teine matuas.
We have always just been expected
to be women.

Postscript

I've always felt attached to the narratives of the Pacific and I've
always felt attached to my roots in the 267, Rewa, Auckland. Being a
daughter of powerful speakers, I always feel like I am an orator before
I am a writer, so my poems are always written to be said aloud, and it
feels more comfortable that way, mainly because there's an exchange
of emotions when performing so I don't always feel the magnitude
of my vulnerability. This poem is rooted in my homes: the Pacific,
Soufside and my nana Falelima Tuiloma. A thank you to all the Samoan
daughters who grew to be the backbone of a family, our mothers.

Lana Te Rore

A Letter to My Younger Self

Dear younger self . . .

Don't be too cheeky,
I would tease
my siblings.
They got the hiding,
not me.
I get on better with my sisters
and siblings,
although some still hold grudges.

My dad would sing
Pearly Shells to us
before bedtime.

My father suffered depression.
So do I,
And my twin sister.
I encourage her not to give up hope.
We encourage each other.

I love you Lana,
hope you don't make the same mistakes I did,
my dad would say.

I make my family laugh,
I enjoy being a clown.
I make everyone laugh,
I don't like seeing people sad.

When I see sad people,
I cheer them up.

I feel very happy
when Mum and Dad get along —

DON'T FIGHT
I yell,
STOP ARGUING.

When they carry on,
I get upset.
I am healing
all the time
from this pain.
I am a survivor of domestic violence and verbal abuse.

My husband and I
are still together,
but live in separate houses

We get on better that way.

I encourage people in life,
no matter where they come from.

We are all unique and special,
and everyone has a gift to offer.

With the talents and abilities we have,
we can go places.
I want to make a difference
in my life and other people's lives,
to go back to study,
and working in the mental health field.

I want to help
make people believe in themselves
and to love themselves
again.

I love myself more
and more each day,
and encourage myself,
and strengthen myself,
and have faith in myself.

I encourage others
to not make the same mistakes
I have made in my life.

I am not that person anymore,
I am changed,
and I am not that angry person anymore.

To do with my husband,
I had to realize
only God can change people.
I can be there for him,
but I don't have to live
with his bouts of anger anymore.
I praise God every day.
How well I have been coping with things.

Teresia Teaiwa

AmneSIA

get real
we were always
just stepping stones
erich von daniken
saw the footprints of the gods
chris connery
saw the trademarks of capitalism
who's gonna give a damn if they don't/can't remember
that the whole of the donut is filled with coconuts
they're after american pie in the east
and some kind of zen in the west
east and west are of course relative
the rim of our basin
is overflowing with kava
but the basin of their rim
is empty
they take their kava in capsules
so it's easy to forget
that there's life and love and learning
between asia and america between
asia and america
there's an ocean
and in this ocean
the stepping stones
are
getting real

porirua market with susanna and jessie, 2009

too early in the morning for jessie
but she manages to smile
we go to market in porirua
to bring kanaky closer

susanna loves the polynesian music and the bustling brown
breakfast is donuts from patelisio's stand — five for a dollar
we get tea, milo, coffee from the māori guy selling his boil-up
beef on sticks from a malaysian stall
we sit, eat, sigh in unison

noa and jessie giggle at a street preacher — thin young pālagi man
susanna recounts emails recently received
a nephew has died
he had taught her how to plant yams
had given her hope for the next crop — next generation

let's try a rhizome theory of revolution:
tuaine asks 'what are you doing here?'
and i say 'this is home'

at porirua market we buy vegetables and fruit, fish, flowers
yes, cash passes from hand to hand
and we do drive back to wellington
but this is a kind of pilgrimage
and we show devotion to the
shouldertoshoulderbustlingbrown and theblareofzipso
that can bring kanaky closer

past struggles worth each bead of brine each bloody tear
because here you can meet bernard narokobi

who wrote his country's constitution
and is as humble now as he was when he wrote it

so we think of yams even as we purchase red potatoes
for this rhizome theory of a revolution that will not be commodified
but humanized and realized in the next crop — next generation

jessie and noa giggle
their mothers smile
not too early: on time

Tulia Thompson

The Girl that Grew into a Tree

She is flimsy as the rippled moon on water
(Her face too, is half-moon and sallow)

in a red silk kite dress.
Her centipede spine curls against vinyl seats.
The rain hides   her short talk   with corrugated iron.

Rising
she drops her wineglass   (a glass slipper)

and waits   to be sewn up.

I am afraid her back will break
before the weight   of her prophecy

bridges her vertebrae to the sky —

They say bird-girls like her don't fly
/ don't change   their feathered   ways.

But next time I see her,

She is cutting flesh   thin   from mango
skin
Lines   in her brown   stretching   out   to ancestors

They say the roots of the tree anchor   as far   underground

As branches that reach to the sky.

Joshua Toumu'a

Veitongo
After Kaveh Akbar

The bakery flows with the scent of rainwater.
A fresh loaf is split in two, it gushes rainwater.
The iron roofing ripples with rainwater.
You cut your leg upon it, it bled rainwater.
Rainwater flows through the air conditioner.
The plastic piping carries rainwater to the concrete tank,
Which is made of rainwater itself.
A louvre slides out of its frame,
Its shards are rainwater.
Rainwater is buried under hot stones and tarpaulin.
Children run across the road to buy rainwater for their family;
They are rainwater themselves.
Rainwater rings through the air on a Sunday morning.
Aunties and uncles laugh loudly, passing around rainwater.
Their laughs are overflowing with rainwater.
Subwoofers in car boots ooze rainwater.
The machete is taken to a coconut,
Rainwater rushes out of it.
I sent you a poem before the waves took out communications.
My words were rainwater.

Rhegan Tu'akoi

Emails from AirNZ are the bane of my existence

care to reduce your carbon footprint?

all my unread emails are from AirNZ
clogging my inbox the way their fuel
chokes our rivers

read on to find out how we're stabilising emissions for environmental benefit

forests of sustainability reports are printed
& promise to reach targets that
AirNZ could've reached yesterday

the koru features on all these documents
as though it's a partnership with kaitiaki
but like the treaty
they want Māori signatures & symbols not input

our coffee cups are made from plants / not plastic

once i leafed through the inflight magazine
it chronicled their annual green morning
a swanky breakfast on the windy waterfront

they awarded themselves a trophy
for sustainability
heads nodded hands clapped
but they still flew planes to every port

only $3.99 to offset your upcoming flight . . .

a billion dollar company
asking me
a student who cuts mould off dollar bread

their footprint's bigger than Bigfoot's
but a clean green future is my choice
so each time i fly
i need to tithe

we! care! about! protecting! the! land!

surely Air New Zealand
should be paying to
offset colonisation

my peers are pale

my peers are pale even though it's summer
we sit in a see-through room on the library's highest floor
beyond the glass is New Zealand history, law & legislation
and maps charted by men who stole our Oceanic coasts

i tug my hangnails when they discuss
economic policies that tax me'akai off tables
and how rheumatic fever is the responsibility of brown parents
and ridiculous bills that advocate for rehabilitation not punishment
and people like me

i don't know why my bones are always up for debate

do they disagree with the composition of my blood
or the way it continues flowing even if police demand it stop
they fraction my ancestors into authentic and plastic
do they not know that our veins have always been brimming
with mango juice & the 'oseni & koka tree dye

ink stains my fingers as i write down their words
but the pages remain blank
colonisation runs up my arm but doesn't seep in
i only have shallow scratches of what we've lost

there are so many stairs to get to the top floor of the library but i walk
them anyway

Tamara Tulitua

tagi mai le taika

I am sitting, with my older sister, against the gym studio wall playing with my Day and Night Barbie. The Jazzercise class is five rows full, synth and guitar riffs are keeping the hype as high as the leotard waistlines. Leg warmers grip pulsating calves, and sweatbands hug big bold perms. My sister and I sit so that Mum is in our line of sight, in her favoured black leotard and hot-pink tights combination. Her long plaited hair seems rebellious amongst the bushy coifs.

'Eye of the Tiger' plays and my sister doesn't flinch — her Peaches and Cream Barbie is getting ready for a dinner party. The instructor is working up to a frenzy. I stand up, hold Barbie so she watches too. Leg kicks! 5, 6, 7, 8. Punches in the air in time to the hook — punch (rest) jab, jab, jab (rest) jab, jab, jab (rest) double jab, then triple-time punching upper hooks, sprinting on the spot. Eye of the tiger!

It's the final sprint and I am transfixed. The leg warmers are running hard on the spot, with big hair rebelling under the sweatbands. Hard breathing, panting, the instructor is screaming now — she's holding out — 'Here we go ladies! This is what we're going for! Let me hear you roar!' Barbie and I scream at the top of our lungs.

Josua Tuwere

Every poem
For Teresia Teaiwa

Every poem is a memory, every rhyme has a face
Every line has a story, every word has a place
Every whisper has an echo, every breath,
Every sinew, every nerve, every ounce
Explodes on the page
Every writer has a muse, every pen has a fuse
Every moment has a record, every page has a turn
Every dance has a journey, every step has a plan,
Every clock has a pace, every timer has a race,
Every ship has a sail, every sailor has a fear,
Every wave has a reason, every wind has a season,
Every word has a sword, every edge has a spill
Every peak has a champion, every down has an up
Every fear has an antidote, every heart has a beat
And us gang, as we so beat, let us so explode
So that every poem has a sword
And every word has a place
And every memory has a sea
That we can still sail on

Losalini Tuwere

Tanoa

T — Taloca mai
A — Au karamaca dina
N — Na wai ni vanua au diva
O — O solia mai me'u gunu mada
A — A! Maca! Qai cobo sara

T — Serve a kava drink!
A — To quench my thirst
N — With the drink of the land, I yearn for
O — Give me, that I may drink
A — Drink with fulfilment to the very last drop!

Tipesa Victoria Samuel Ulavale
My aunt's song

I am playing with my dog
outside my aunt's fale.
I hear her singing inside her house
while she is weaving a mat.
I feel the spirit of her song.
I see her cry, but I don't want
to ask her why.

I hear the last line of her song.
'Ia e pei o le toloa pe lele i
Fea ae ma'au lava i le vai.'
'We have to be like the grey duck.
Wherever the grey duck flies
it always goes back to the water.'
For Samoan people, wherever we go,
we will always go back to
the place where we belong.

Now I understand
why she sings and cries.
I'm leaving her soon.
I start to cry too.

Ailine Vakasiuola

Loloma from 3pm–4pm

3:00pm
Her classroom filled with future housewives
Thick hair parted straight down the scalp,
both Merida and Rapunzel's plaited neatly in two.
Ring, ring, ring
Six long blue pleats saturated in dried starch
Sprint across the school yard
The sharp stones stapled to the bottom
of her scruffy sandals mark each stride

3:15
Sweaty elbows shoved against hers,
Torn leather seats and stained-glass windows
Shades of blue, green and red fill a bus.
Silent glares pierced to the back of her mind
Daring not to catch the eyes of the green schoolgirl.
A ticking time bomb

3:30
Her sweaty hands grip the cold metal bars of *Lui's* dairy
Two big brown eyes gazing through another
at green and gold plastic wraps,
fats and sugars rare to the tongue
'e ha?   So what will it be?
Her tippy toes are sacrificed for a glimpse of the fridge
Overdosed on soda, tip top and water bottles.
Flirtatious smirks of the sun mean nothing but harm,
as survival she chooses
                    Just a Cola please

3:40
She wraps her lavalava around her waist
Pinches the ends and ties it neatly in a knot,
Sunset printed Gardenia perfectly paints her figure.
She takes the last sip of her Cola then shoots it
across the room shouting
>   *Kobe!!*

she straps a tea towel to her shoulder,
and so the routine begins.
Dust
Sweep
Shine
Chop
Slice
Fry
Wipe,

4:00pm

Māhina T. Valentine

View from the summit of an Island named after an extinct bird

Bird of Prayer — Hone Tuwhare

A circus of beauty
    streaks across sunset
        luminous wings
            cresting the curve
                of Sugarloaf
      two kāhu are calling
          calling as they helix
              high   into Sky
           they intertwine like fibres
        of a long fishing line
             like the invisible
        umbilical that binds us
to everything: Life!
    slips unhindered
  from my lips
      & air
   flowing in freely
they say   the heart is a muscle
           to strengthen
   with oxygen
a gift
   and a promise

Kasi Valu

Ipu Tī

Uncanny faces circulate the mattresses and chairs I call home
Outside are 8 pairs of slippers, inside there are 3 couches
The jandals painted white on the brown balm of each sole, ribboned with
red and blue leather straps

I've seen these ones at Otahuhu, they sell them next to the Talo
I've seen my Nena wear this to the flea market
I've seen my Nena swing this like a helepelu slicing wild spring onions
when my brother gets lippy

Yesterday was Saturday,
I know because I can smell baked talo leaves and the juice of plums
wedged between slats of dough
Excommunicated hands get slapped for reaching, the answer is no
I woke up to the hum of prayers shifting the couches around
Nena tells me to boil the kettle, and plate the super wine biscuits,
she winks at me to save the Krispie coconut cookies for later

Everyone in the lotofale pouts their lips and scratches the air like a wild cat,
encouraging me to kiss them
I see no point in doing so but they insist
I only do so for the Krispie coconut cookies waiting for me in shelf above
the microwave
Only Nena can reach them so I have to be good
2 tablespoons, not teaspoons of sugar
Chelsea commands mills that toss and turn the sap of sugar canes
blowing in the humid breeze across salty waters
My Nena told me our people were traded like sheep to farm the seeds for
Chelsea, just for us to have sugar in our cups
That's why it's two tablespoons

The scent of the room is confusing
A concoction of musky cologne
Coconut oil
Warm ashy feet
Victoria's Secret body lotion & mist
Nena beams her eyes,
Cutting through the glass cabinet
Adorned with family photos that partition the kitchen and the lounge
I return the Bell tea box into the cupboard
Wistfully scamper to the kettle and open the glass jar compressed with
Twinings, earl grey

Everyone prefers their tea without milk
Pure black tea
The universe wanted to conspire trials to test the emptiness of my stomach
Volcanic branding on my wrist masked by a searing smile if I trip over
the Fala
I remember last time it burned my hand, I popped my bubble too early
and it got infected
I had to stay in my room, I couldn't leave the house

Tulou is your safe word, passing through valleys of whispering aunties
with bulging eyes
Passing through shiny bald heads lathered in Nivea cream & Joop
The men sit on the floor, their legs crossed like crispy caramel pretzels
A man holding an apple green rosary stretches his leg out like a tired
vine screeching for the warmth of the sun
Pivot, swivel, head down, smile and the safe word
The Patele is served first, he sits on my Grandpa's chair,
Nobody is allowed on that chair,
It's like trying to re plant a hibiscus in winter,
Nobody is allowed to sit in my Grandpa's chair
My smile fades
Ika'i!

Have I done something wrong?
The safe word, it must be my smile
Twinings?

The Patele smiles and speaks with his eyes
I nod my head and serve the woman perched on the couches
Dressed in assortments of black lace, embellished with flowers foreign to
the soils of my Nena's garden
Emulating the curtains that decorate each window sill

Marked with crimson red lipstick that sticks to the hairs on my cheek
like candle wax
I am loved beyond measure
I glide with grace back to the microwave with my price towering above
my head

I wait
They begin singing my favourite song
I feel mafana
My feet begin to melt and my eyes swell with tears
The cupboard creaks open, it required cautionary care with the rusty
iron screws that barely hold the box together
I feel lips barbed with cactus thorns pressed against the top of my head
My grandpa towers over the rivers that stream down my face
He hands me the Krispie coconut cookies
Nena's last packet saved for me, a taste that transports her home in one bite

'Aho ni

Sāpate
Today I woke up to the sun gleaming through the crevices of mouldy curtains
The sky mirrored the ocean that connects you to me and me to you
Clear as night, bright as day
Today I woke up to the hum of cicadas calling,
Beckoning
Singing to find their families
Waves of humidity enamoured with hope wash over the shorelines edging
the fences that once stood strong against any current
Today I woke up to the quaking of the Earth's mantle
My Nena's photo hung alone in the centre of the lotofale
The Virgin Mary face flat scattered in a pool of glass
Today I woke up to conglomerates of ash mounted on the sills of every window
The sky mirrors the flags that remain raised to galaxies unbeknownst to
contrite hearts that beat for the voice of our people
Feathers of faith galvanise the skin of my aunty's gold tooth, our beacon
through the night, navigating refuge in what is still our paradise
My home becomes a speck from the top of the mountain
Around me, remains what is immeasurable
There standing, the hope and dreams of my ancestors
There standing, the beacon through the night
There standing, our people
And they are resilient as the immovable coconut tree dancing to scathing
and raging winds that attempt to batter and bruise the essence of its treasure
Awaiting a new dawn
Awaiting our ancestors' call
Awaiting the rise of the sun to melt the ice caps buried in the wells of our souls
Though the Earth has cracked and the sky has fallen, our people still rise

Jonah Vili
Your tangi

Tears falling in Kaikohe
find passage downstream
over river stone altars that
bless the feet of mountains
Beauty of untouched forest
I see beyond mellow fields
Your aunties tell me   you
would gather watercress there

Hot pools spray mist
over crest of your marae
Your brothers stand stoic
as the cemetery walls
that guard your mother
The chapel tolls waiata
with your sons' voices
resonating in karakia

Under Ngawha skies
of cloudy pastures
I stand above   you
tending to our trees
Our girl weeps beside me
watching you descend
She knows   you
will not return

Our boy in his suit
kneels on the mound
ushering the earth
onto your vessel

He lies on his back
making earth angels
Whanau are amused.
'That's his Hāmoa side.'

A man with a shovel
looks annoyed and
walks towards our boy
'Let him bury his mother,'
I say with alofa
His eyes acknowledge
with surprise — then sadness
as he strokes our boy's face

Our girl stands still
on edge of your grave
Her tears fall in hymn
with the returning soil
Our boy joins his brothers
to challenge the gods
with your haka.
He is laughing with the sun

'Is Mummy sleeping, Daddy?'
He does not know   you
will not return
Our girl now stirs
'No. She's dead, aye Daddy?'
Trying to stem their tears
they wait for my answer
to comfort their hearts

But I am carved in thought
My tongue is Kauri
My eyes are shells
My heart is stone
In a graveyard sowed with death
I am captured —
by how full of life
the weeds are

Jahra Wasasala

The World-Eater & the World-Shaper

truthfully, there is no greater horror than being born.

at this moment, I speak to You with half a body.
I am still collecting the rest, but there is enough of Me here to be visible
just as these words on this page are visible to You.

this half-body won't be able to satiate me for much longer.

so, before *You* and *I* become *We*
I will tell You the rules;

SAIVA:
this body is not (y)ours and They are/I am asking for it back.

DUA:
I am not a living thing. nor am I a dead thing. You are not a living thing,
nor a dead thing. remember this.

RUA:
there is more than one world. there is more than one memory. each
maintains their own laws, their own first fall from the sun, their own
approaching descent into madness. each sees through their own eyes.

TOLU:
I am sewn together through purified will.
an aggregation of ruins,
possessed.
I moulded myself. I drew the borders around the beginnings and endings
of my body
but I do not abide by any of them.

VA:
I am named before every loss.
I am named after every inheritance.
I am named in the vein
of what I am entitled to:
Dra.

>–+–<

as We are about to begin, it is already over
the sky has been burnt and blackened, filling Our mouth with ash and song

We hear it first
the sound of a tear in the fabric of this universe. the sound of laws being
broken.

the tear that is made creates a living, pulsating wound
in time.
the wound opens like the universe's eye, scanning, surveying
unblinking, it begins to emit a disembodied scream scream scream
scream scream scream scream scream scream scream scream
scream scream scream scream scream scream scream
polluting the sky.

the Scream itself, like a liquid
pouring out of the wound, wrestling with its own form
a cluster of natural disasters adorned in a caliginous embryonic fluid
a ball of heat and light begins to form itself in the centre of the Scream
transforming into a force of *Yalo*, electricity, and semi-translucent matter

resisting the form
resisting the borders
the Scream's embryonic womb bursts with the pressure

the Scream is growing a head

then another

and another

sitting atop long writhing necks, the faces emerging on the armoured heads are never fixed.
if you think you can identify one, it mutates into something unrecognisable.
there is a face, and yet there is none. there is a body, and yet there is none.

The Scream rapidly crawls across the horizon like a lizard, tainting everything it touches. the Scream is deliberate, dutiful, relentless looking for Us.
The Scream knows Our scent, no matter what mask We choose within whatever fleshy apparatus We are possessing.

The Scream stops their rampage across the sky. one of their heads catches Our eyes.

then another.

and another.

the air between Us and Them turns acidic.
a brief moment of acknowledgement

the multi-headed voice makes their way towards Us,
a body, gaining lifetimes in speed,
a body, carving a horizon bloody
jaws unhinging at the joints like old gates,
dragging the sky into the ground as they open.

We resist.

the closer The Scream gets,
the more We are pulled in
the more We are a collapsing star
being dragged into a blackhole.

We resist

giving The Scream the charge it needs to begin The Breaking.

We resist

Our made-human-body surrenders
flesh howling
as it tears itself away from the bone,
the marrow within starting to boil
and leak, forming sacs of fluid erosion that corrupt
an already corrupted body

this should hurt.
this kind of pain should be enough to tear any embodied psyche apart.
this should be the kind of pain We have dreamt about.
but that does not matter
We cannot register any pain, because We are facing the only thing that We
are afraid of; [redacted]

attempting to escape doesn't help.

inhale.

the only thing that can be done is bracing on impact.

>—+—<

The Breaking done to Us happens within a moment. but this moment
defies time-score,
holding Our multiple lifetimes hostage.

The Scream collides with Our made-human-body
wrapping its semi-translucent form around Us. the collision is
so violent that
within this moment it swallows sound.
for the first time since The Scream emerged from the wound in the sky, it
settles on a single face.

The Scream's voices slither into Our ears,

'You have gone too far.'

'there is only one way.'   *'Your rebellion follows you like a stench.'*
'there is no one left to hold up the sky.'

'Dra . . . forgive me.'
'how many did you consume?'
'eater of worlds! the masked clown! answer!'
'the only language you know is thirst.'

expecting resistance, The Scream grows four disjointed, yet human-like,
arms and claws.
grabbing onto Our face, The Scream uses their new appendages to break
open Our human jaw
forcing themselves inside / a ghost crawling down Our throat.

nestled inside Our human-made-body, The Scream is expanding
a bomb exploding in slow-motion, pushing against Our forged human walls
until they cry with terror.

still, We resist.

The Scream unwraps its centre and buries it within Our spine
it begins to rupture and explode Our human-made-body is suddenly filled
with the light and sound of a dying star thousands of years of trauma
beginning and ending folding and splitting everything We have seen and
bodied every dream and nightmare all at once the force of light and sound
racing around our human-made-body is excruciating and cruel We hate
this We hate this We are enveloped burning with the scent of death and
shame We had carefully sewn Ourselves into this human-made-body but
those stitches have melted apart leaving the flesh and Us vulnerable and
unbound the eyes We found and loved melt out of their sockets and We are
made blind again the lungs We found and loved burst into dust choking Us
from the inside out get them out get them out get them out

The Scream uses its arms to pull itself out of Our mouth.
as they leave, Our exterior body follows them, peeling itself away in fragments.
Our true being, the unpredictable,
volatile and fragile form of many faces, is left
exposed. We are a rupturing world of torment and failure
this naked-being becoming a whip of rage,
lashing out at anything within reach

No.
Not now.
Not again.
We were so close.

shrieking and begging and wailing and demanding
We grab at the bone fragments, memory and flesh that have been
stripped from Us, trying to will them
back into something We can speak through.
(a splintered oesophagus. a loose jaw bone. wiring from a nervous
system. blood and ash pooling in Our voice.
that will do. that is enough to possess, for now).

We smell the cold scent from The Scream.
turning to face them, We speak in Our shared-tongue,

'The Scream and We were named together! Yalo and Dra! do you not
remember?!'

The Scream watches, silent and motionless.

The Breaking has left Us convulsing so violently that words crack and
fall to the ground as they are spoken.
what is remaining of Our rotting human-made-body falls to the ground,
hissing as it slowly disintegrates.

'We were so close this time . . . please.'

The Scream watches, silent
and motionless.

>—+—<

The Scream gently begins reversing their movements,
crawling backwards on its belly across the sky.
　　their heads retracting back into The Scream's first form of storms,
　　　　the embryonic fluid sealing it whole
　　　　　until they are called upon again.
The Scream quietly slips back into the living rupture it was birthed from

　　　　　the universe's eye,
　　　　an open witness to The Breaking,
　　　　　closes,
　　the wound sealing itself as if nothing had been seen.

>—+—<

I spit out the ash and blood pooling in my throat until I am empty.

it is done.
I have been broken.
disembodied.
abandoned.

good.

I pull *the clown*'s mask out of Our remains
stitching it lovingly to where a human head of mine might be

laughing
as I begin to fill in the features with My chaos.

exhale.

We, are starved.
We, are loved.

let's begin.

again.

>—+—<

Albert Wendt

Incantation

Over the Waitakere the sky darkens and darkens
In its belly the faint blink of lightning
Barely audible thunder a few seconds later
Then thick rivulets of rain weave down
the bare branches of the kowhai beside him
Isabella Te Wera Tehaaora Hohepa Ashley Tahu Sina
Caleb Moengaroa Amelia Orlando Maika
His mokopuna's names slip sparkle and burn in
the heart of his tongue an incantation
which lifts him above the storm
He turns his palms upwards
but the storm doesn't care to read them
Storms happen and the kowhai loses its leaves
according to the pacing and intention of the seasons
What is there at the end of leafing?
Some of his mokopuna will grow into prophetic readers
some will stumble early into the irresistible darkness
some will help wash and prepare his body for cremation
Outside his umbrella cover he extends his hands
Icy raindrops tattoo his palms but he can't read the patterns
The caves along the rugged range of his history
are stacked with carefully labelled files of loved ones
and the intruders he can't exile into oblivion:
His father in his khaki work clothes is suddenly beside him
whispering 'the storm has no power and will end shortly'
Fundamentalist faith eyeless analysis and courage had been
his father's basis of navigation with an all-knowing God
as central pivot of the Star Map he had made them all live by
until he was in the ultimate court and he couldn't decipher
in speech his Map's purpose and the dawn of the second coming
His mother has been a decisive eloquence over the sixty years since

she died of cancer and became his most precious presence
Always he has desired her understanding of the heart's
whispering darkness and her acceptance of the future
and the unhealable pain of separation
The dark above the Waitakere has melted away
The rain has ceased but his hands are numb with cold
The bare branches of the kowhai are sleekly black with wet
The choice is to be here with his mokopuna and parents
The continuation is that of alofa and forgiveness
Isabella Te Wera Tehaaora Hohepa Ashley Tahu Sina
Caleb Moengaroa Amelia Orlando Maika
Luisa Tuaopepe . . . the incantation will continue
to shape soothe and unread his present

Into the First Cold

1.

Once his sight and bones didn't know the four seasons
He was born into Samoa's two seasons of wet and dry
and the air's wrap that rarely dropped below 22 degrees
The lush forests did not ever shed their green
and crops sucked up the soil's precocious blood all year round

No need for fur or other animal skin or fabric
Apt nakedness was adequate clothing for the times
despite the Victorian taboo of covering from neck to toe
Not one inch of erect skin shine to be exposed
Sex was only for procreation and in the sin-chocka dark of night

2.

His first taste of ice water was a shocking burn around his teeth
then round his mouth and down his gullet and chest
as a long-nailed finger that scraped up choking tears
Ice cream was the only cold he loved but his family couldn't afford it
He learned about snow and ice from books and films

Across the Pasefika on the banana boat out of the sun's cling
into a cold that seeped down into his marrow and wouldn't let go —
a journey from warm ease into seasick body crunched up
in his first ever woollen clothes and shoes the seas and skies turning
wilder darker predicting a New Zealand locked in the loneliness of cold

3.

First at boarding school under cone-perfect Taranaki beanied
with ice snow and tapu the cold and homesickness gripped his every bit
The teachers ordered early morning runs and cold showers afterwards
to toughen the will against the invading winter and shape them
into men who wouldn't flinch from any kind of pain

Rugby and military drill were the other manly prescriptions
Twice weekly rugby practice and the game against another school and winter
Tackle and tackle attack and attack the pain was exhilarating and beat
the cold and forged the ideal team that would die for one another
Winning wasn't everything — it was the only thing

Military drill in prickly uniforms with his courage as steely as the rifle
he carried erectly at the epic school parades with their much medalled
headmaster in splendid command and some of his teachers mimicking
the decorated heroes they'd been in the Second World War others with silence
refusing to glorify the futile leap into colonial wars' insatiable gobs

Left-right left-right left-right halt! Young fit acclimatised he now lived
comfortably with the cold weather and being away from home
But every morning when he walked in Taranaki's compass to breakfast
the mountain signalled not all was well with the path
His history teacher praised Te Whiti's stand at Parihaka

He researched that and discovered almost 200 years
of settler invasion fraud and theft of iwi land
A deadlier cold slid into his throat and held him hostage
to an anger as rich as Taranaki's beauty and defiance
of colonialism injustice and greed behind the eyes

And so it is

we want so many things and much
What is real and not? What is the plan?

Our garden is an endless performance
of light and shadow quick bird and insect palaver

The decisive wisdom of cut basil informs everything
teaches even the black rocks of the back divide to breathe

Blessed are the flowers herbs and vegetables
Reina has planted in their healing loveliness

The hibiscus blooms want a language to describe their colour
I say the red of fresh blood or birth

A lone monarch butterfly flits from flower to flower
How temporary it all is how fleeting the attention

The boundary palm with the gigantic Afro is a fecund nest
for the squabble of birds that wake us in the mornings

In two weeks of luscious rain and heat our lawn
is a wild scramble of green that wants no limits

Into the breathless blue sky the pohutukawa
in the corner of our back yard stretches and stretches

Invisible in its foliage a warbler weaves a delicate song
I want to capture and remember like I try to hold

all the people I've loved or love
as they disappear into the space before memory

Yesterday I pulled up the compost lid
to a buffet of delicious decay and fat worms feasting

Soil earth is our return our last need and answer
beyond addictive reason fear and desire

Despite all else the day will fulfil its cycle of light and dark
and I'll continue to want much and take my chances

Gem Wilder
Unfurled

Hillsy found a kurī skin,
tightly rolled and brittle,
in the basement of a Wanganui museum
back before the h was returned.

He built it an acid-free kennel,
put in a saucer of distilled water
that he kept topped up
as if the dog could lap at it,
and waited,

as patient as the kurī itself,
standing on the prow of a waka
on that long journey,
a living figurehead,
anticipating landfall
when it would finally have
enough space to unfurl.

Faith Wilson

I'm out for dead presidents to represent me

My words ain't worth shit
and since I was a girl I was told
to put my money where my mouth is.

As a brown kid in Aotearoa it was all bout
dem dollar dollar bills yo, even though they

became defunct in '91.
Before I was born, I was a nickel
in my mother's ovaries and a dime
in my dad's moneybags.

You could even say I'm made of money.

I'm your two-dollar coin
golden and baby oil shiny:
slip me into your slot machines

I'm your tatty fiver
a regular mountain climber

I'm voting for the Mana Party
with your tenner

I'm fucking Queen Elizabeth
I'm decolonising your fiddy

Preparing you for nuclear
fallout on your C Note

'Cos my words ain't worth shit
but I know how to spend my body
I'm made of money and I'm burning
bullet holes in your pockets.

Bah Humbuck

Sweating in a colony
in the sun

sit Nana's humbucks:
see through plastic Glad bag
into red & tan

Humbucks she calls them.

FOB speak; lingua franca
Humble sweet; Scrooge was a wanker

We drive in her car with
too much dangly shit hanging
from the rearview mirror —
they chatter when we turn corners.

Dashboard Jesus —
pray for us.
He's stuck down with old
peppermint Freedent.

(I have all the God I need in this car)

I never know where we're going
I ignore how fast we're going
I just trust her hair
a silver (grey) aura
in this South Waikato sun.

I suck & suck & suck
my humbuck
til the sharp bits cut
my tongue:
red & tan.

And then I crunch it.

Nana can only suck
let it roll around her
flabby inner cheeks

Minty fresh; lolling tongue
Sweet & false; teeth and gum

We turn up
Englebert
Elvis
Frank
Bing

They speak for us.
I don't care when eyes
from other cars glare
when we stop at the red light,
wondering why a young afakasi
and a silver bunga lady
are blasting music
played by old white dudes.

I just stare back, picking
flotsam & jetsam
sugar & corn syrup
the humbucks left in my teeth.

(I have all the holy I need in this car)

We hoon
120
. . . 130
. 140
says she can't feel the speed
creeping up on her.

It doesn't matter anyway —
(Saint Christopher, pray for us)

I rip off my seatbelt and
throw my head out the window,
screaming the lyrics
until my voice is as loud
as the wind.

Nana holds my hand,
crosses herself with her right
when we pass the church
so for a few seconds
only God is steering.

We're almost there I think,
so I distract Nana, hoping she'll drive
past and forget.

I want this ride to go on forever.
And ever.
Amen.

Glossary

adi	chiefly title used for women of high rank (Fijian)
afakasi	of mixed ethnicity (Samoan)
'aho 'ni	today (Tongan)
aiga	family (Samoan)
aitu	god or spirit (Samoan)
aiuli	theatrical dancing around a central figure being honoured or celebrated (Samoan)
ali'i	chief or leader (Samoan)
alofa	love (Samoan)
aloha	greetings, welcome or love (Hawaiian)
aloha 'āina	strong sense of connection to the land (Hawaiian)
alu ese	leave, get away, take off (Samoan)
ata mai	clever, smart (Samoan)
Atea	sacred ancestor (Cook Islands Māori)
au	special implement made of bone used in ceremonial tattooing (Samoan)
Aukilani	Auckland (Samoan)
bu	ripe coconut (Fijian)
bubu	grandmother (Fijian)
bullkaka	crap, bullshit (urban slang)
bure	thatched hut (Fijian)
dadakulaci	non-venomous banded sea-snake (Fijian)
davui	conch shell trumpet (Fijian)
dra	blood (Fijian)
dua	one (Fijian)
'E ha?	What would you like? (Tongan)
'enua	land (Cook Islands Māori)
fa'a Sāmoa	way of life, Samoan culture
fa'afafine	identifying as gender-fluid or non-binary (Samoan)
fa'afetai	expression of gratitude, thanks (Samoan)
fa'alavelave	cultural practice of giving money at large family occasions such as funerals, weddings and significant birthdays (Samoan)

fa'alifu fai'i	side dish of green bananas cooked in coconut milk (Samoan)
fa'amolemole	polite request (Samoan)
fa'atama	gender-fluid or non-binary (Samoan)
fa'atuatua	faith (Samoan)
fạiảkse'ea ma ạlạlum	formal expression of thanks and gratitude (Rotuman)
fala	mats woven from pandanus leaves (Samoan)
fala paongo	woven mat of high value (Samoan)
fale	building designed in traditional architectural style (Tongan)
fale aitu	theatrical ghost or spirit (Samoan)
fale o'o	small house or family dwelling (Samoan)
falema'i	hospital (Samoan)
fanua	land, earth (Samoan)
fie-vale-loi	pretend not to know, to act dumb (Tongan)
filemu	tranquil, serene (Samoan)
fileteado	style of Argentinean decorative graphic art
Fitiuta	name of a village in American Samoa
fofō	massage (Samoan)
fonua	land (Samoan)
fue	ceremonial fly whisk carried by a chief as symbol of authority (Samoan)
gafa	family tree, genealogy, whakapapa (Samoan)
gafatele	having Samoan ancestry
gogo	seagull (Samoan)
Guåhan	original name for Guam in the language of the indigenous Chamorro people
haharạgi	young or emerging (poets) (Rotuman)
Hāmoa	Sāmoa (Māori)
haole	foreigner (Hawaiian)
helepelu	type of knife (Tongan)
Hinenuitepō	goddess of the night (Māori)
hula	dance (Hawaiian)

ie lavalava	wraparound cloth worn as dress or skirt by both men and women. 'Ie' means sheet or piece of fabric; 'lavalava' is the style of wearing it (Samoan)
ihi	essential force or personal magnetism (Māori)
ika'i	no (Tongan)
ipu tī	cup of tea (Samoan)
kai valagi/vulagi	foreigner, stranger (Fijian)
kaikamahine	daughter (Hawaiian)
Kanaky	ethno-political name for the island of New Caledonia
Kenese	Genesis (Samoan)
Keriso	Christ (Samoan)
koko alaisa	Samoan cocoa rice dish
koko Sāmoa	Samoan drinking chocolate
koloa	fine mats (Tongan)
kūpuna	grandparent, ancestor (Hawaiian)
la calle	street (Spanish)
lagituaiva	ninefold heavens of the supreme god Tagaloa; 'lagi' means heavens and 'iva' means nine (Samoan)
lalolagi	humanity, humankind (Samoan)
lei	garland (Hawaiian)
lelea' mafua	mature, senior (Rotuman)
lima	five (Samoan)
limu	seaweed (Hawaiian)
lotofale	community mental health facility (Samoan)
mafana	being friendly, hospitable (Samoan)
ma'i	sick (Samoan)
mainese	pink potato salad dish (Cook Islands Māori)
makona	hard, mean, implacable (Samoan)
mākutu	witchcraft, sorcery (Māori)
malo 'aupito	thank you (Tongan)
malofie	traditional full-body ceremonial tattoo worn by men (Samoan)
malosi	strong (Samoan)
malu	traditional ceremonial female tattoo (Samoan)

mamoe	Samoan-style stir-fry dish
mana	life force (Māori)
manaia	spirit-world messenger with bird-like beak (Māori)
manavā	breath (Samoan)
manu	bird, beast (Samoan)
manumea	*Didunculus strigirostris*, tooth-billed pigeon, Sāmoa's national bird
manuvuka	small bird (Fijian)
māsū	wheeze (Samoan)
Mau Sāmoa	political movement for Samoan independence from colonial rule
mauga	mountain (Samoan)
meʻakai	food (Tongan)
mele	song (Rotuman)
miti	coconut cream sauce (Fijian)
moetolo	literally 'sleep crawler', sexual predator (Samoan)
moʻoku ʻauhau	whakapapa, genealogy (Hawaiian)
na vale	home (Fijian)
nena	nana, grandmother (Tongan)
ngaue	work (Tongan)
ngeru	cat, feline (Māori)
Niu Sila	New Zealand (Samoan)
Oʻahu	Hawaiian island
ʻohana	family (Hawaiian)
ʻoka	raw fish dish (Samoan)
ʻoseni	ocean (Tongan)
ota	fern (Fijian)
papalagi	foreigner, non-Samoan
pasese	fare (Samoan)
patele	priest, chaplain, pastor (Samoan)
Pele	goddess of volcanoes (Hawaiian)
pēpē	baby, babe (Samoan)
pepelo	false, fake, fraudulent (Samoan)
poke	chopped-up and mixed food dish incorporating seafood and salad (Hawaiian)

pouliuli	darkness (Samoan)
pulotu	underworld, abode of the gods (Samoan)
Ra'iātea	island in French Polynesia
Rohe	goddess of the night (Māori)
rua	two (Fijian)
rukau	baked taro leaves (Cook Islands Māori)
saiva	zero (Fijian)
sami	sea, seas (Samoan)
Sāpate	Sunday, the Sabbath (Tongan)
sausau	tattooing mallet (Samoan)
Savaiki	fabled homeland (Cook Islands Māori)
siusiu pipi	cooked turkey tail (Samoan)
siva/siva Sāmoa	Samoan dance
soa	family member who is getting a pe'a or malu traditional tattoo at the same time as you are, sharing the ceremony (Samoan)
sole	casual term of address meaning bro', dude or man (Samoan)
suka	sugar (Samoan)
ta'ahine	miss, young woman (Tongan)
ta'avale	car (Samoan)
Taema	one of the matriarchs or goddesses of tatau (tattoo) (Samoan)
taiaha	long-handled wooden fighting staff (Māori)
Tagaloa	the strongest Samoan god
tala	dollar (Samoan)
talanoa	discussion, meeting, hui (Fijian, Samoan, Tongan)
talo	taro (Tongan)
talofa	greetings, welcome, hello (Samoan)
Tama-Nui-Te-Rā	Great Son of the Sun (Māori)
tama'ita'i	lady, woman (Samoan)
tạn kạlu	round water, puddle (Rotuman)
tanoa	kava bowl (Fijian)
taonga	treasure, inheritance, object of sacred value (Māori)

tasi	one (Samoan)
tatau/tatatau	tattoo (Samoan)
tātua	belt (Māori)
tauiwi	people who are not Māori, especially non-indigenous New Zealanders (Māori)
tauʻolunga	traditional Tongan dance
taupou	ceremonial hostess, leader of the unmarried women of the community, who welcomes distinguished visitors (Samoan)
tau-sami	eat (Samoan)
Te Ariki	Paramount Chief (Cook Islands Māori)
Te Fiti	Mother Earth (Hawaiian)
Te Ka	fire demon (Samoan)
temamfua	elders, ancestors (Rotuman)
teine lelei	good girl (Samoan)
teine matua	grown-up girl (Samoan)
teitei	plantation (Fijian)
tiare apetahi	rare emblematic flower from the Tahitian island of Raʻiātea
tiare māori	gardenia (Cook Islands Māori)
Tilafaigā	one of the twin sisters who brought the art of tatau (Samoan tattoo) to Sāmoa
tinā	mother (Samoan)
tino	body (Samoan)
tivaevae	patchwork quilt sewn communally (Cook Islands Māori)
tolu	three (Samoan, Fijian)
toto	blood (Samoan)
totō	to burp, belch (Samoan)
totolasi	multi-ethnic heritage (literally 'of many bloods') (Samoan)
tufuga	master tattooist (Samoan)
tulafale	orator (Samoan)
tulou	excuse me (Samoan, Fijian, Tongan)
tumeke	startled or excited (Māori)

tupenu	skirt-like garment wrapped around the body (Tongan)
uce	gender-specific term used when a man addresses a man who is not a blood relative as brother, or when a woman addresses a woman who is not a blood relative as sister (see also **uso**) (Samoan)
ula	funny (Samoan)
'ulu	breadfruit (Samoan)
upu	word(s) (Samoan)
uro-ni-vonu	breadfruit (Fijian)
uso	brother or sister within an extended family. This term is gender-specific, meaning it can be used among men or among women, but never between men and women. Men can call each other uso, but a woman cannot. Women can call each other uso, but a man cannot (see also **uce**) (Samoan)
va	four (Fijian)
vā/va	pan-Pacific concept denoting relationships between people and things in the natural world
vaka	canoe (Cook Islands Māori)
vanua	land (Fijian)
vasa	ocean (Samoan)
Veitongo	village on the main island of Tongatapu in Tonga
vinaka vakalevu	thank you very much (Fijian)
waka hourua	double-hulled sailing canoe (Māori)
wananavu	wonderful (Fijian)
wehi	awe, amazement (Māori)
yalo	heart, life-force (Fijian)
Yap rai	large carved circular stones once used as currency on the Micronesian island of Yap (Yapese)

Bibliography

Most of the poems in this anthology have been previously published in books, journals and other locations. We are grateful to their publishers and other copyright-holders for giving their permission to reproduce them in *Katūīvei*.

Alefosio, Marina. 'Raiding the Dawn'. *The Coconet*, www.thecoconet.tv/moana-arts/coco-performance/raiding-the-dawn-poem-by-marina-alefosio

——— 'The Local Theatre'. *Catalyst* 11 (2014).

Aolani, Aziembry. 'Name'. *Ora Nui: Māori Literary Journal* 4 (2021), New Zealand & Taiwan Special Edition.

———'Parking Warden'. *Turbine | Kapohau* (2000), https://turbinekapohau.org.nz/archive-issues/2020-contents/poetry-aziembry-aolani

Avia, Tusiata. 'Ova-sta-ya' and 'We are the diasporas'. *Fale Aitu: Spirit House*. Wellington: Te Herenga Waka University Press, 2016.

——— 'Poly kidz r coming'. *The Savage Coloniser Book*. Wellington: Te Herenga Waka University Press, 2020.

Barford, Serie. 'Hearts and sensitive grass' and 'Say my name without the "sh"'. *Entangled Islands*. Wellington: Anahera Press, 2015.

——— 'Into the world of light'. *Sleeping with Stones*. Wellington: Anahera Press, 2021.

Brown, Pelenakeke. 'Crossings'. Created for the exhibition *Mana Moana, Mana Wāhine*. Raven Row Gallery, London, 2019.

Brown-Pereira, Audrey. 'who are you, where you come from, where you been your ( )hole life?'. *a-wake-(e)nd*. Auckland: Saufo'i Press, 2023.

Campbell, Maringikura Mary. 'Dreams' and 'Savaiki'. *Yellow Moon | E Marama Rengarenga: Selected Poems*. Auckland: HeadworX, 2020.

Carter-Bennett, Denise. 'Hēninuka'. *Vā: Stories by Women of the Moana*. Auckland: Tatou Publishing, 2021.

Case, Emalani. 'On Being Indigenous in a Global Pandemic'. *Indigenous Pacific Islander Eco-Literatures*, edited by Kathy Jetñil-Kijiner,

Leora Kava and Craig Santos Perez. Honolulu: University of Hawai'i Press, 2022.

Christopher-Ikimotu, Hele. 'Dear Banaba'. *No Other Place to Stand: An Anthology of Climate Poetry from Aotearoa New Zealand*. Auckland: Auckland University Press, 2022.

——— 'Unknown'. *Blackmail Press* 38 (2014), www.blackmailpress.com/MTHI38.html

Cole, Gina. 'His Majesty O'Keefe'. *Exploring Multicultural Poetry: Book Two*, edited by Vaughan Rapatahana. Invercargill: Essential Resources, 2019.

Eggleton, David. 'Flying In, Southside' and 'The Great Wave'. *Edgeland and Other Poems*. Dunedin: Otago University Press, 2018.

——— 'Lifting the Island'. *Landfall* 237 (2019).

Esau, Amber. 'Liminal'. *NZ Poetry Shelf*, https://nzpoetryshelf.com/2021/11/29/poetry-shelf-monday-poem-amber-esaus-liminal

——— 'Street Fighter'. *Skinny Dip: Poetry*. Auckland: Massey University Press, 2021.

Eteuati, Sisilia. 'Denial'. *Blackmail Press* 36 (2014), www.blackmailpress.com/Index36.html

——— 'Island Girl'. *Landfall* 234 (2017).

Faamanatu-Eteuati, Niusila. 'For the learners of Gagana Sāmoa — O se fa'amanatu mai le Matāmatagi'. *Vā: Stories by Women of the Moana*. Auckland: Tatou Publishing, 2021.

Fepulea'i-Tapua'i, Aigagalefili 'Fili'. '275 Love Letters to Southside'. *Poetry New Zealand Yearbook 2019*. Auckland: Massey University Press, 2019.

Fepuleai, Maureen Mariner. 'Mum, where are you?'. *Love from the Indigenous Queen*, edited by Maureen Mariner Fepuleai. Auckland: iQ Talanoa Trust, 2020.

Fesola'i, Sunema. 'Passage to Paradise'. *One Behind the Eight-ball: A Collection of Short Stories and Poems*. Paekākāriki: Earl of Seacliff Art Workshop, 2023.

Filisi, Helen Tau'au. 'Mana whenua o Māngere'. *Mana Māngere Voices*, edited by Helen Tau'au Filisi. Auckland: Helen Tau'au Filisi, with support from Māngere-Ōtāhuhu Local Board, Auckland Council, 2017.

Fonongaloa, Kalisolaite. 'Untitled'. *Le'o'o Pasifiki*, edited by Feana Tu'akoi.

Palmerston North: Palmerston North City Council, Square Edge Community Arts and Massey University, 2022.

Ford, Tere Takurangi Kathy. 'New Shoes'. *Te Kinakina: E Ngara i te Ngari: Remember Where You Come From, Stories from Cook Islanders in Tokoroa*, edited by Vaughan Rapatahana. Wellington: Read NZ Te Pou Muramura, 2021.

Gray, Tim. 'Homeless of the heart'. *More than a Roof*. Wellington: Landing Press, 2021.

Hack, Rob. 'Despite Meena', 'Cannons Creek Four Square' and 'All day on Maʻuke'. *Everything Is Here*. Wellington: Escalator Press, 2017.

Iwashita-Taylor, Grace. 'Dear South Auckland'. *The Pantograph Punch* (2020), www.pantograph-punch.com/posts/dear-south-auckland

——— 'Queen Street Stroll'. *Ika* 2 (2014).

——— 'Tinā | Mother'. *Afakasi Speaks*. Honolulu: Ala Press, 2015.

Jenkins, Caitlin. 'South'. Winner of the International Institute of Modern Letters (IIML) National Schools Poetry Award, 2021, https://schoolspoetryaward.co.nz/2021/08/11/south-caitlin-jenkins

Kaho, Simone. 'Half' and 'Jam'. *Lucky Punch*. Auckland: Anahera Press, 2016.

——— '. . . young families, with children.' *HEAL!* Auckland: Saufoʻi Press, 2022.

Kamali, Daren. 'Coconuts don't grow here'. *More than a Roof*. Wellington: Landing Press, 2021.

——— 'Duna Does Otara'. *Landfall* 225 (2013).

——— 'Manteress'. *Squid Out of Water: The Evolution*. Honolulu: Ala Press, 2014.

Latimer, Mereana. 'PLASTIC pēpē PLASTIC'. *Sweet Mammalian* 7 (2020).

Lavasʻi, Kristoffer. 'What Remains to Be Seen'. Unpublished.

Lavea-Timo, Daisy. 'Fringe Dwellers'. *Catalyst* 15 (2018).

Lehuanani, Mary. 'Limu'. *More of Us*. Wellington: Landing Press, 2019.

Lemalu, Schaeffer. 'im'. Unpublished.

Letoa-Paget, Rex. 'Zapelu Kidz'. *Tupuranga Journal* 1 (2019), www.tupurangajournal.com/rex-paget

Leupolu, Luana. 'Aeroplanes'. *Mayhem Journal* 6 (2018).

——— 'A Poem I Didn't Think to Write'. *Mayhem Journal* 4 (2016).

Lim-Cowley, Luka Leleiga. 'Straightening Out'. *Statis* (2020).

Macomber, Ruby Rae Lupe Ah-Wai. 'Storytelling'. *Starling* 5 (2018).

Maiava, Ole. 'Can you see me?'. Unpublished.

Manoa, Ioana Yule. 'History'. Winner of the International Institute of Modern Letters (IIML) National Schools Poetry Award, 2016, https://schoolspoetryaward.co.nz/category/2016-award-winner

Marsh, Selina Tusitala. 'Dinner with the King'. *Tightrope*. Auckland: Auckland University Press, 2017.

——— 'Entering Pouliuli'. *Takahē* 100 (2020).

——— 'Girl from Tuvalu'. *Dark Sparring*. Auckland: Auckland University Press, 2013.

Masae, Ria. 'Vinyl Sundays A-Track', 'Mā', 'Gripping sand'. *AUP New Poets 7*. Auckland: Auckland University Press, 2020.

Meredith, Courtney Sina. 'The internet told me to go for a run'. *Burst Kisses on the Actual Wind*. Auckland: Beatnik, 2021.

——— 'Brown girls in bright red lipstick'. *Brown Girls in Bright Red Lipstick*. Auckland: Beatnik, 2016.

——— '"How about being a woman"'. *Ko Aotearoa Tātou: We Are New Zealand*. Dunedin: Otago University Press, 2020.

Meredith, Kim. 'Dance of Sina'. *Ika* 4 (2016).

——— 'Love Letters from Glen Innes'. *Ko Aotearoa Tātou: We Are New Zealand*. Dunedin: Otago University Press, 2020.

Mila, Karlo. 'Touch in the age of COVID'. *Love in the Time of COVID* (2021), https://loveinthetimeofcovidchronicle.com/2020/08/01/touch-in-the-age-of-covid-karlo-mila

——— 'Tūhoe Boys' and 'After Reading Ancestry'. *Goddess Muscle*. Wellington: Huia, 2020.

Nasau, Sakaraia. 'I Miss You'. *Voqa Ni Veisemati: Vola Italanoa Ni Viti e Aotearoa*, edited by Sai Lealea, Losalini Tuwere and Moira Wairama. Wellington: Read NZ Te Pou Muramura, 2021.

Pamatatau, Richard. 'Language'. *Ko Aotearoa Tātou: We Are New Zealand*. Dunedin: Otago University Press, 2020.

——— 'Cuisine rules'. *Six Pack Sound*. Auckland: New Zealand Electronic Poetry Centre, 2019, www.nzepc.auckland.ac.nz/features/six-pack-sound/08/pamatatau.asp

Peaua, Mele. 'My journey'. *Somewhere a Cleaner*. Wellington: Landing Press, 2020.

Pili-Tavita, Niavā. 'My mother is like no other'. *Love from the Indigenous Queen*, edited by Maureen Mariner Fepuleai. Auckland: iQ Talanoa Trust, 2020.

Poole, Doug. 'Tuailemafua'. Unpublished.

——— 'The light I had hoped'. *Ika* 4 (2016).

Pule, John. 'I try to leave with the sun'. *Artspeak*. Vancouver: Artspeak, 2022.

——— 'to end my voice with time, space and sea . . .' *Still not close enough*. Auckland: Gow Langsford Gallery, 2021.

——— 'Looking at rain too long has given me eternity'. First performed on film shown at COP27, Sharm el-Sheik, Egypt, 2022. Managed by SPREP, Sāmoa, for Mana Moana Pasifika Voices.

Purcell Kersel, Nafanua. 'Modesty Tasi, Lua, Tolu', and 'Face Recognition'. *Vā: Stories by Women of the Moana*. Auckland: Tatou Publishing, 2021.

Rands, Melanie. 'when the boat comes down'. *Scope Journal: Border Crossings: New Dialogues in Pacific Art & Design* (November 2012).

——— 'Banana Poem'. Unpublished.

Raymond, Rosanna. 'Pulotu Pollution'. *Blackmail Press* 34 (2013), www.blackmailpress.com/Index34.html

Richards, Luti. 'Papa'. *I am my Father's Eulogy*. Self-published chapbook, 2022.

Rodger, Victor. 'Sole to Sole'. *Skinny Dip: Poetry*. Auckland: Massey University Press, 2021.

Ruddy, Anne Hollier. 'Song of the Islands'. *More of Us*. Wellington: Landing Press, 2019.

Sauvao Pasene, Luaipouomalo Naomi. 'To Be a Samoan Woman'. *The Guerrilla Collection*, 2022, https://theguerrillacollection.nz/poetry-spoken-word-competition-2022-winner-naomi-sauvao

Sale, Saulaina. 'The Poet'. *Mana Māngere Voices*, edited by Helen Tau'au Filisi. Auckland: Helen Tau'au Filisi, with support from Māngere-Ōtāhuhu Local Board, Auckland Council, 2017.

Soakai, Dietrich John. 'Untitled'. *Blackmail Press* 34 (2013), www.blackmailpress.com/Index34.html

Soakai, Eric. '298 Urban Orators' and 'Forgive Yourself'. Unpublished.

Soakai, Zech. 'A Streetcar Named Diaspora'. *Red Room Poetry* (2019), https://redroompoetry.org/poets/zech-soakai/streetcar-named-diaspora

Solomone, Fesaitu. 'Fantabulous Blackie'. Unpublished.
So'oula, Sala'ivao Lastman. 'Blackbird'. *Blackmail Press* 45 (2022), www.blackmailpress.com/Index45.html
Strickland, Onehou. 'Dusky warrior'. Unpublished.
Strickson-Pua, Rev. Mua. 'Hip Hop Tag 2013' and 'Williamson Ave to Scanlan Street'. *Blackmail Press* 39 (2015), www.blackmailpress.com/Index39.html
Tafuna'i, Faumuina Felolini Maria. 'I am Sieni' and 'Hulk for a Day'. *My Grandfather Is a Canoe*. Christchurch: Flying Geese, 2021.
Taito, Mere. 'no frills'. *Landfall* 230 (2016).
——— 'taṇ kaḷu'. *More of Us*. Wellington: Landing Press, 2019.
——— 'the quickest way to trap a folktale'. *Manifesto Aotearoa: 101 Political Poems*. Dunedin: Otago University Press, 2017.
Taito, Ruana. 'Our fale'o'. *More than a Roof*. Wellington: Landing Press, 2021.
Talo, Elizabeth. 'If I knew then what I know now / Poetic lemonade' (originally titled 'If I knew then what I know now'). *The Guerrilla Collection*, https://theguerrillacollection.nz/poetry-spoken-word-directors-choice-winner
Tamatoa, Matafanua. 'Sunday Best'. *Landfall* 233 (2017).
——— 'Organics in Ōtara'. *Landfall* 240 (2020).
Tamu, Leilani. 'Researching Ali'i'. *Landfall* 231 (2016).
——— 'Aotearoa Runaway' and 'Paradise Pasifika'. *The Art of Excavation*. Auckland: Anahera Press, 2014.
Taufa-Vuni, Mepa. 'Feasting the eyes'. *The Art of Excavation*. Auckland: Anahera Press, 2014.
Tauri-Tei, Luisa-Tafu. 'Teine lelei'. *Sweet Mammalian* 6 (2019).
Te Rore, Lana. 'A Letter to My Younger Self'. *Rough Lives Speak*, edited by Daren Kamali and David Eggleton. Street Poets and Artists Collective Enterprise (SPACE), 2022.
Teaiwa, Teresia. 'AmneSIA'. *Sweat and Saltwater: Selected Works*. Wellington: Te Herenga Waka University Press, 2021.
——— 'porirua market with susanna and jessie, 2009'. *Blackmail Press* 36 (2014), www.blackmailpress.com/Index36.html
Thompson, Tulia. 'The Girl that Grew into a Tree'. *Blackmail Press* 34 (2013), www.blackmailpress.com/Index34.html

Toumuʻa, Joshua. 'Veitongo'. Winner of the International Institute of Modern Letters (IIML) National Schools Poetry Award, 2022, https://schoolspoetryaward.co.nz/2022/08/18/veitongo-joshua-toumua

Tuʻakoi, Rhegan. 'Emails from AirNZ are the bane of my existence'. *No Other Place to Stand: An Anthology of Climate Change Poetry from Aotearoa New Zealand*. Auckland: Auckland University Press, 2022.

——— 'my peers are pale'. *Stasis* 2 (2021).

Tulitua, Tamara. 'tagi mai le taika'. *The Pantograph Punch* (2022) .

Tuwere, Josua. 'Every poem'. Unpublished.

Tuwere, Losalini. 'Tanoa'. *Voqa Ni Veisemati: Vola Italanoa Ni Viti e Aotearoa*, edited by Sai Lealea, Losalini Tuwere and Moira Wairama. Wellington: Read NZ Te Pou Muramura, 2021.

Ulavale, Tipesa Victoria Samuel. 'My aunt's song'. *More of Us*. Wellington: Landing Press, 2019.

Vakasiuola, Ailine. 'Loloma from 3pm–4pm'. *Mayhem Journal* 9 (2021).

Valentine, Māhina T. 'View from the summit of an Island named after an extinct bird'. *Love in the Time of COVID* (2021), https://loveinthetimeofcovidchronicle.com/2020/12/04/recital-of-poems-9-mariana-isara-valentine-mary-cresswell-gregory-dally-danielle-todd-miriama-gemmell

Valu, Kasi. 'Ipu Tī'. Unpublished.

——— "Aho ni'. *The Big Idea* (2022), https://thebigidea.nz/stories/speaking-from-the-soul-celebrating-aotearoas-poets

Vili, Jonah. 'Your tangi'. *Ika* 3 (2015).

Wasasala, Jahra. 'The World-Eater & the World-Shaper'. Unpublished.

Wendt, Albert. 'Incantation'. *Cafe Reader* 15 (2017).

——— 'Into the First Cold'. *Takahē* 91 (2017).

——— 'And so it is'. *Indigenous Pacific Islander Eco-Literatures*. Honolulu: University of Hawaiʻi Press, 2022.

Wilder, Gem. 'Unfurled'. *Sport* 43 (2015).

Wilson, Faith. 'I'm out for dead presidents to represent me'. *Sport* 43 (2015).

——— 'Bah Humbuck'. *Blackmail Press* 41 (2015), www.blackmailpress.com/Index41.html

About the poets

Marina Alefosio is a New Zealand-born Samoan writer who has worked for over a decade with poetry, spoken word, script writing and music. She has performed at the Nuyorican Poets Café in New York, the Adelaide Fringe Festival and the Dawn Raids Apology Ceremony. She won two artist residencies with Banff Creative Arts Institute and Tautai Pacific Arts Trust, and has been published in *Catalyst 11*, *IKA* and *RAPTURE: An Anthology of Performance Poetry from Aotearoa New Zealand*. She is studying towards a Master's in Indigenous social change through the University of Melbourne.

Aziembry Aolani (Ngāpuhi, Kanaka Maoli) is a writer and gamer. He is a former student of Victor Rodger at the International Institute of Modern Letters, Te Herenga Waka Victoria University of Wellington. His work has been published at Toi Māori Gallery, in *Ora Nui*, *Turbine* and the *Food Court* zine.

Tusiata Avia MNZM is a New Zealand-born Samoan. Her poetry collections, published by Te Herenga Waka University Press, include *Wild Dogs Under My Skirt* (2004), *Bloodclot* (2010), *Fale Aitu | Spirit House* (2016), *The Savage Coloniser Book* (2020) and *Big Fat Brown Bitch* (2023). *The Savage Coloniser Book* won the Mary and Peter Biggs Award for Poetry at the 2021 Ockham New Zealand Book Awards. Two of her poetry collections have been turned into notable stage productions which have toured nationally and internationally.

Serie Barford was born in Aotearoa to a German-Samoan mother (Lotofaga) and Pālagi father. She held a 2018 Michael King Writers Centre Pasifika residency, and performed at the 2019 international Book Arsenal Festival in Kyiv. Her poetry collection *Sleeping with Stones* was shortlisted for the Mary and Peter Biggs Award for Poetry at the 2022 Ockham New Zealand Book Awards.

Pelenakeke Brown is an interdisciplinary artist whose practice explores the intersections between disability theory and Samoan concepts. She has published writing, undertaken residencies and presented performances in New York, California, Berlin, Hamburg, London and Aotearoa. She has been profiled in *Art in America* and recognised with a Creative New Zealand Pacific Toa Award.

Audrey Teuki Tetupuariki Tuioti Brown-Pereira's poetry collections include *Threads of Tivaevae: Kaleidoskope of Kolours* (Steele Roberts, 2002) with Veronica Vaevae, *Passages in Between I(s)lands* (Ala Press, 2014) and *a-wake-end* (Saufo'i Press, 2023). She has performed at the New Zealand Fringe Festival and Poetry Parnassus in London. Born in the Cook Islands and raised in Aotearoa New Zealand, Audrey lives in Sāmoa with her family. She is a graduate of the University of Auckland and the National University of Sāmoa.

Maringikura Mary Campbell lives in Pukerua Bay in the old family home with her whānau. She is the mother of three sons and four mokopuna. Identity, loss, tūpuna and wairua are common themes in her writing. She is not a prolific writer, but rather writes when a poem is given or there is a fire in her belly.

Denise Carter-Bennett is a wahine writer and poet of Māori and Kanaka 'Ōiwi whakapapa. She lives in Tāmaki Makaurau Auckland with her tama and ngeru and works as a cybersecurity engineer.

Emalani Case is a Kanaka Maoli writer, teacher, and aloha 'āina deeply engaged in issues of Indigenous rights and representation, colonialism and decolonisation and environmental and social justice. She is the author of *Everything Ancient Was Once New: Indigenous Persistence from Hawai'i to Kahiki* (2021). She is from Waimea, Hawai'i.

Hele Christopher-Ikimotu is of Niuean, Banaban and I-Kiribati descent. A proud Pacific Islander and South Aucklander, his writing is inspired by the communities that birthed and raised him as well as everyday interactions and experiences.

Gina Cole is a Fijian, Kai Valagi writer who lives in Tāmaki Makaurau Auckland. Her collection *Black Ice Matter* (Huia, 2016) won the Hubert Church Best First Book Award for Fiction at the 2017 Ockham New Zealand Book Awards. Her work has been widely anthologised and published. She holds a PhD in creative writing. Her novel *Na Viro* (Huia, 2022) is a work of Pasifikafuturism.

David Eggleton is a poet and writer of Rotuman, Tongan and Pākehā heritage. His collection *The Conch Trumpet* won the Mary and Peter Biggs Award for Poetry at the 2016 Ockham New Zealand Book Awards. He also received the 2016 Prime Minister's Award for Literary Achievement in Poetry. David was the Aotearoa New Zealand Poet Laureate from 2019 to 2021.

Amber Esau is a Sā-Māo-Rish (Ngāpuhi/Manase) writer of things from Tāmaki Makaurau Auckland. She is a poet, storyteller and professional bots. Always vibing at a languid pace, her work has been published both in print and online.

Sisilia Eteuati is a poet, writer and lawyer who has a Master's in creative writing from the University of Auckland. Sisilia is the co-founder of Tatou Publishing and has worked as a lawyer in Sāmoa, Australia and Aotearoa. Her work has been published in various places across the Pacific, including *Landfall*, *The Sapling*, *Blackmail Press*, *Samoa Observer* and *Samoa Planet*.

Tavuʻi Niusila Faamanatu-Eteuati is the Dean of the Faculty of Education at the National University of Sāmoa. She is also an adjunct research fellow of the School of Languages and Cultures at Te Herenga Waka Victoria University of Wellington. Niusila has worked as an education and language lecturer for over twenty years at tertiary institutions in Sāmoa and New Zealand. She has published, translated and edited children's books, and written short stories, poems and academic articles in education research, teacher education and environmental studies. She is married to Leiataua Joe, has a twenty-year-old old son, Johanius Alailima Faamanatu, and she hails from the villages of Samusu Aleipata, Vaegā Satupaʻitea, Solosolo and Manono Sāmoa.

Aigagalefili Fepulea'i-Tapua'i is a Samoan poet and climate change activist. In 2019 she organised Pacific climate change collective 4 Tha Kulture and participated in the 2019 climate strikes. She was awarded the Young Leader Award in the New Zealand Women of Influence Awards in 2020.

Maureen Mariner Fepuleai was born in Sāmoa but raised in Aotearoa. As a firstborn, she has had many family responsibilities which she continues to honour. She draws creative inspiration and energy from motherhood. She describes herself as tama'ita'i Sāmoa and a Southside Aukilani citizen.

Sunema Fesola'i is a writer and poet who was born in Tāmaki Makaurau Auckland, where her Samoan parents arrived in the 1950s. Her paternal connections are to the village of Faleasi'u in Upolu, and her maternal connections are to the village of Vailoa in the district of Palauli, Savai'i. Her extended family grew up in and around the Pacific Island Presbyterian Church in Newton, Auckland. She lives in central Auckland, where she has raised her family of three sons.

Faalavaau Helen Tau'au Filisi is a Samoan/New Zealand mother, author, educator and creative who lives in Māngere, South Auckland. She is completing a PhD at Te Whare Wānanga o Awanuiārangi, and counts as a blessing her beautiful Samoan parents, her children and her Samoan culture.

Kalisolaite Fonongaloa is of Tongan descent. She is a student at Palmerston North Girls' High School. She loves reading, writing, playing instruments and sports.

Tere Takurangi Kathy Ford is a first-generation New Zealand-born Cook Islander who calls Tokoroa, New Zealand, home. Tere hails from the Islands of Tongareva, Aitutaki, Aitu, Mangaia and Palmerston. She was born in the early 1970s to Rimarau and Toreakore Rima-kainga-e-te-Mango (nee Tekena Marsters) Ford. They migrated to New Zealand for a better way of life, coerced by the 'land of milk and honey'. Tere was raised on a multicultural street where everybody called you by name, where everybody welcomed you at their table, where everybody treated you as their own.

Tim Gray is a New Zealand-born Samoan with German and Chinese roots. He has worked as a banker, a print journalist, a market researcher, a cleaner and a labourer.

Rob Hack was born in Invercargill and is of Cook Island and Kiwi heritage. He had an awesome childhood on Niue and after several forays around Australia now lives on the Kāpiti Coast. He runs two weekly creative writing classes at Te Ara Korowai in Raumati Beach and hosts a monthly radio show on Te Pae called *Not at the Table: Poetry and Stuff*. He is researching and writing about the life and times of Papa (Sir) Tom Davis.

Grace Iwashita-Taylor is an artist of upu/words and has Samoan, English and Japanese bloodlines. She was a recipient of the CNZ Emerging Pacific Artist Award in 2014 and the Auckland Mayoral Writers Grant in 2016. Grace held an international writer residency at the University of Hawai'i in 2018. She is author of the collections *Afakasi Speaks* (Ala Press, 2013) and *Full Broken Bloom* (Ala Press, 2017) and is co-editor of *RAPTURE: An Anthology of Performance Poetry from Aotearoa New Zealand* (Auckland University Press, 2023).

Caitlin Jenkins is a poet of Tongan (Fatai village), Niuean (Toi village) and Pākehā descent. She is studying towards her certificate and qualification in hairdressing. In 2021 she won the International Institute of Modern Letters National Schools Poetry Award with 'South', a poem that celebrates the diverse cultural histories of South Auckland.

Simone Kaho (Tongan, Pākehā) has a Master's in poetry from the International Institute of Modern Letters. She directed *E-Tangata*'s *Conversations* web series and has reported for *Tagata Pasifika*. Simone's first poetry collection is *Lucky Punch* (Anahera Press, 2016) and her second book, *HEAL!* (Saufo'i Press, 2022), is about recovery after sexual violence.

Daren Kamali is of Fijian, Uvean, Futunan, Samoan and Scottish ancestry and lived in Fiji for his first seventeen years. He is a multimedia revivalist, research artist and poet. He says, 'Poetry for me connects the past to the present — old to the new, sea and islands, heritage and contemporary.'

Mereana Latimer (Ātiu, Pākehā, Ngāti Apa, Ngā Wairiki) was born and raised in Te Whanganui-a-Tara. Her writing has appeared in *Turbine / Kapohau*, *Sweet Mammalian*, *Takahē* and on stage, with thanks to Prayas Theatre.

Kristoffer Lavasiʻi is a Samoan New Zealander (from the villages of Vaigaga, Saleʻaula and Musumusu) with connections to Switzerland, Ireland and Scotland, and was born and raised in Ngāruawāhia. This is his first time being published.

Daisy Lavea-Timo is a New Zealand-born Samoan (Saipipi, Vailuʻutai, Samatau) poet whose work is deeply rooted in her ancestry and her role as a tulafale (orator chief). Daisy's writing explores her identity as a product of the Samoan diaspora and strives to communicate ideas about complex societal issues connected with culture and leadership.

Mary Lehuanani Togoiu Misiki came to Aotearoa New Zealand from Apia, Sāmoa, in 2017. She attended Aotea College in Porirua, and now lives in Tāmaki Makaurau Auckland. She wrote her poem 'Limu' in 2018.

Schaeffer Lemalu (1983–2021) was a Lebanese/Samoan painter and poet. He was the author of the chapbooks *sleeptalker* and *sleeptalker2* as well as many folios of unpublished poems. A posthumous collection of his writing is forthcoming from Compound Press.

Rex Letoa-Paget (Samoan/Danish) is a faʻafatama crafter of words who was born in Aotearoa. His poetry is his compass through space and time, as he journeys through loss, grief and shame that have been learned growing up in a colonial society as part of the Pasifika diaspora. His writing offers lessons, learnings and acknowledgments to the traditions of yesterday, today and tomorrow.

Luana Leupolu grew up in Ōtāhuhu, Auckland, the youngest in a musical family of Samoan-European background. She studied music and creative writing at Te Whare Wānanga o Waikato the University of Waikato, during which time she was first published in *Mayhem Journal*.

Luka Leleiga Lim-Cowley is a totolasi London-born Samoan poet and disinclined PhD candidate. Their work usually ends up having something to do with Pacific Indigenous self-determination, gendersexuality divergence, disability justice, anti-racism, climate justice and abolition.

Ruby Rae Lupe Ah-Wai Macomber is a proud diasporic daughter of Te Moana-nui-a-Kiwa. Her whakapapa stretches from Rotuma to Taveuni, Kaikohe and Tāmaki Makaurau Auckland, where she now lives. When Ruby is not writing, she is a Te Kāhui creative writing facilitator, law student, Pacific studies researcher and advocate for her community.

Ole Maiava is an artist and performer, as well as a published poet and short story writer, with credits in scriptwriting and radio plays. He is a first-generation Aotearoan and a forty-third-generation Samoan on his mother's side. He helped establish Auckland's annual Pasifika Festival in 1993, and has also served as its director.

Ioana Yule Manoa is a Samoan woman in her twenties who lives and works in Tāmaki Makaurau Auckland. Her featured poem was written when she was in year 12 at Northcote College and it won the 2016 National Secondary Schools Poetry Award. She is now a graduate engineer, specialising in structural engineering.

Selina Tusitala Marsh ONZM, FRSNZ, of Samoan and Tuvaluan ancestry, is a former New Zealand Poet Laureate and has performed poetry for primary schoolers and presidents (Barack Obama), queers and Queens (Elizabeth II). She has published three collections of poetry with Auckland University Press: *Fast Talking PI* (2009), *Dark Sparring* (2013) and *Tightrope* (2017), and an award-winning graphic memoir, *Mophead* (2019), which was followed by *Mophead Tu* (2020) and *Wot Knot You Got? Mophead's Guide to Life* (2023).

Ria Masae is of Samoan descent and was born and raised in Tāmaki Makaurau Auckland. Her work has been published in various national and international literary outlets, including *Landfall, Cordite, Circulo de Poesía* and *Best New Zealand Poems* (2017 and 2020). In 2020 a collection of her poems titled 'What She Sees from Atop the Mauga' was published in *AUP New Poets 7*.

Courtney Sina Meredith is an Auckland poet, playwright, fiction writer and musician. Of Samoan, Mangaian and Irish ancestry, she is the former director of the Tautai Pacific Arts Trust and an honorary fellow in writing at the University of Iowa. Her award-winning works include the play *Rushing Dolls* (Playmarket, 2012), the poetry collections *Brown Girls in Bright Red Lipstick* (Beatnik, 2012) and *Burst Kisses on the Actual Wind* (Beatnik, 2021), and the short story collection *Tail of the Taniwha* (Beatnik, 2016).

Kim Meredith is a multimedia artist, writer and journalist of Samoan heritage. She edited *Burst Kisses on the Actual Wind*, the poetry collection from Courtney Sina Meredith (Beatnik, 2021). She heads the Moana-owned and Moana-led Kim Meredith Gallery in Tāmaki Makaurau Auckland.

Karlo Mila MNZM is a Pasifika writer and poet of Tongan (the villages of Kolofo'ou and Ofu), as well as Samoan and Pākehā descent. Her first collection, *Dream Fish Floating* (Huia, 2005), won the NZSA Jessie Mackay Best First Book Award for Poetry at the 2006 New Zealand Post Book Awards. She has subsequently published two further poetry collections, also with Huia: *A Well Written Body* (2008) and *Goddess Muscle* (2020).

Sakaraia Nasau says: 'Bula Maleka! Na yacaqu o Sakaraia. Au gone ni Vutia, Rewa. I'm a typical Fijian teenager, who loves playing sport, particularly rugby and hanging out with friends. Writing is not my favourite thing, but it's cool. I draw inspiration from my family for my writing.'

Richard Pamatatau is an emerging poet fascinated by the slippery intersection of space, place and class. As a former journalist, poetry has given him the chance to be more playful with facts and ideas to challenge assumptions about identity and belonging. He teaches creative writing at Auckland University of Technology.

Mele Peaua came to Aotearoa New Zealand from Tonga in 1987 and started work as a cleaner on the day she arrived. She has been cleaning or sewing ever since. From 2004 she has been active in the union movement. She has six children, and lives in Lower Hutt.

Niavā Pili-Tavita is of Samoan descent and was raised in Tāmaki Makaurau Auckland; she was the first in her family to make it to university. She is a high school teacher of maths, science and chemistry and has taught in New Zealand and Australia. Niavā says, 'In the midst of Covid-19 my mother was battling stomach cancer in Auckland. The world came to a standstill — I couldn't travel over from Melbourne to care for her. "My mother is like no other" is about fond memories of stories my mother would tell us.'

Doug Poole is of Samoan heritage. His poetry has been included in the anthologies *Niu Voices: Contemporary Pacific Fiction 1* (Huia, 2006), *Mauri Ola: Contemporary Polynesian Poems in English* (Auckland University Press/University of Hawai'i Press, 2010), *IKA Journal of Creative Writing: One* (Manukau Institute of Technology, 2013) and *Indigenous Pacific Islander Eco-Literatures* (University of Hawai'i Press, 2022). Doug is founder and publisher of the online poetry journal *Blackmail Press*.

John Pule has been writing since 1980 and painting since 1984. He has received many awards and honours for his work. Formerly based in Tāmaki Makaurau Auckland, he recently returned to live in the village of his birth, Liku, in Niue. He returns to Aotearoa regularly.

Nafanua Purcell Kersel (Aleipata, Faleālupo, Satupa'itea, Tuaefu) is based in Te Matau-a-Māui, Aotearoa, where she raises three children, many animals and sometimes her voice. A graduate of Te Pūtahi Tuhi Auaha o

Te Ao the International Institute of Modern Letters, she was the recipient of the 2022 Biggs Family Prize in Poetry for her collection *Black Sugarcane*.

Melanie Rands was born in Tāmaki. Her moʻokuʻauhau is to Hawaiʻi, Fiji, Sāmoa, Tongareva and Scotland. She has a fine arts degree from Elam School of Fine Arts and completed her Master's in creative writing at the University of Auckland in 2011. She lives at Matapouri Bay in Te Tai Tokerau with her husband and their dog.

Rosanna Raymond MNZM, New Zealand-born, of Samoan and Tuvaluan descent, specialises in working within museums and higher education institutions as an artist, researcher, curator, guest speaker, poet and workshop leader. Over the past twenty years she has been a notable producer of and commentator on contemporary Pacific Island culture in Aotearoa New Zealand, the United Kingdom and the United States. She is a member of the arts collectives Pacific Sisters and SaVĀge K'lub.

Luti H. Richards is a creative writer, producer, spoken-word poet and self-published author of the autobiography *I Am My Father's Eulogy* (2022). She is co-founder of New Zealand's successful high school poetry slam WORD — The Front Line (2014). She was born and raised in Te Whanganui-a-Tara Wellington and lives in Melbourne, and is a passionate explorer whose roots are proudly in the South Pacific islands of Tokelau and Sāmoa.

Victor Rodger is a writer and producer of Samoan and Scottish descent. As a playwright he is best known for his play *Black Faggot* (2014) and as a theatre producer he has produced Tusiata Avia's *Wild Dogs Under My Skirt* and also her *The Savage Coloniser Show* to critical acclaim. In 2021 he was made an Officer of the New Zealand Order of Merit for services to Pasifika theatre and arts.

Anne Hollier Ruddy's English father and Samoan mother met in Levuka, the old capital of Fiji. They arrived in New Zealand when she was four years old and most of her life has been spent here. Anne's poetry has been published in New Zealand and Australian anthologies.

Luaipouomalo Naomi Sauvao Pasene is of Samoan heritage. She was born in South Auckland and lives in Māngere East. An earlier version of this poem was co-winner of The Guerrilla Collection Poetry/Spoken Word Competition in 2022. She wrote 'To Be a Samoan Woman' to inspire thought and love, while also trying to shine a light on the massive roles Samoan women play in her life.

Saulaina Sale is a poet of Niuean descent who lives in South Auckland.

Dietrich John Soakai is of Tongan, Samoan, German, English, Scottish, Irish and Fijian descent. He is a performance poet and joined the South Auckland Poets Collective in 2011. He has performed his work all around Aotearoa New Zealand as well as internationally. Dietrich lives in Ōtautahi Christchurch with his wife, Hannah.

Eric Soakai is a Samoan (Poutasi Falealili), Tongan (Pangai Haʻapai) artist and poet based in South Auckland. He was the New Zealand Poetry Slam Champion in 2019 and the University of Auckland Poetry Slam Champion in 2021, and his work has appeared in various academic and literary journals including *Knowledge Makers* Vol. 5 (Thompson River University Press, 2020) and *RAPTURE: An Anthology of Performance Poetry from Aotearoa New Zealand* (Auckland University Press, 2023).

Zech Soakai is an award-winning poet who comes from a long line of orators and storytellers. He is of Samoan and Tongan descent with links to both Poutasi, Upolu, Sāmoa, and Haʻatoʻu, Pangai, Haʻapai. When not writing or reading, he likes to spend time with family.

Fesaitu Solomone is of Rotuman and Tongan heritage. Born and raised on the island of Rotuma, she migrated to Aotearoa New Zealand, making her home in Tāmaki Makaurau Auckland in 2006. Her love of writing and deep connection to her homeland Rotuma enabled her to publish her first collection of poems, *My Memories, My Heart, My Love*.

Sala'ivao Lastman So'oula has ancestral connections to the Samoan villages of Fasito'o Uta and Sāfune and grew up in South Auckland. He began writing poetry in the form of rap in his teenage years, later discovering spoken-word poetry and becoming a member of the South Auckland Poets Collective in 2015. His work speaks to lived experiences of urban Pasifika people in Aotearoa New Zealand.

Onehou Strickland is a poet, screenwriter and editor of Cook Island and Māori heritage who made her poetic debut with the South Auckland Poets Collective, focusing on performance poetry and spoken word. Her work with Auckland Museum's *Pou Kanohi* exhibition is where her deep love for and interest in the Māori Battalion began.

Strickson-Pua Gafa whakapapa: Strickson Peterborough Fulham London England, Pua PapaSataua Savaii Sāmoa, Laiman Canton China, Purcell Malaela Aleipata Upolu Sāmoa Ireland France. Ngāti Hamoa Cantonese Saina Irish French Aotearoa Niu Sila born. **Mua Strickson-Pua** is of Samoan heritage and grew up around Ponsonby and Grey Lynn. He began writing political protest poetry in the early 1980s. Reverend Mua Strickson-Pua was ordained as a church minister in 1990. A social worker and activist, he is pioneering co-founder of Street Poets Black, a group of Pasifika poets, dancers, actors, comedians and storytellers. His poetry has featured in many Pasifika publications and anthologies. Dedicated to his great-granddaughter Lacey Grey aka Grey Fa'amanuiaga Atua's Alofa.

Faumuina Felolini Maria Tafuna'i is from Mulifanua and Asaga in Sāmoa. Her poetry traverses the lives of Pacific peoples. Her book, *My Grandfather Is a Canoe* (Flying Geese Press, 2021), has been adapted for the stage, winning multiple awards. Her poems also appear in *Fika, Dried Grass Over Rough Cut Logs, No Other Place to Stand* and *Pacific Voices*.

Mere Taito is a poetry, flash fiction and short story writer and scholar of Rotuman heritage who is based in Kirikiriroa Hamilton. Her work has appeared in *Landfall, Bonsai,* and *Best New Zealand Poems* as well as in academic journals such as *International Education Journal*.

Ruana Taito is Samoan, a mother of five children and the wife of church minister Tomasi Taito, of Livingstone Evangelism Ministries-Maʻaola, Wellington. She has a background in social work and has worked with Counties Manukau District Health Board and non-government organisations in Wellington, and is diabetes community coordinator with Diabetes New Zealand in Porirua.

Elizabeth Talo was born and raised in South Auckland and is of Samoan and Māori descent. Her father's family originates from the villages of Faleasiʻu and Vaiusu in Upolu and her mother is Māori (Ngāti Whātua, Raukawa). Her poem, written when she was a student at McAuley High School, was the poetry/spoken-word competition director's choice winner on the Guerrilla Collection website in 2021.

Matafanua Tamatoa was born in the mountainous village of Saʻanapu, Sāmoa, and spent her childhood in Ōtara, South Auckland. It was there she discovered a love for reading at her local Tupu Youth Library, which eventually led to creating stories of her own. Matafanua spends her time with her aiga and community and she relaxes by watching YouTube shorts.

Leilani Tamu was born in Tāmaki Makaurau Auckland and is a Moana writer of Samoan and Tongan descent. Her work has been published in a range of journals and anthologies, and her first book, *The Art of Excavation* (Anahera Press, 2014), was longlisted for the poetry prize at the 2015 Ockham New Zealand Book Awards.

Mepa Taufa-Vuni is a mother of five children and a proud Tongan descendant who lives in South Auckland. She grew up in Vainī, and Haʻateiho, Tongatapu, and migrated to Tāmaki Makaurau Auckland in 2007. She is a graduate of the University of the South Pacific and the University of Auckland and studies and works at Massey University, Auckland.

Luisa-Tafu Tauri-Tei says, ʻI am the Samoan daughter of where the Pacific meets the shores of Saute Aukilani. I was born and raised here by a line of women who have consistently sacrificed themselves for the hopes of something better. I am the by-product of their love and support, and without it I wouldn't write. Fa'afetai o a'u Tinā.'

Lana Te Rore was born at Waikato Hospital along with her twin sister, Jendy. Her mother, Viriama Tuapou, is from the village of Nikaupara on Aitutaki in the Cook Islands.

Teresia Kieuea Teaiwa (1968–2017) was a poet and scholar of Banaban, I-Kiribati and African-American descent. She taught at the University of the South Pacific in Fiji, and in 2000 moved to Te Whanganui-a-Tara Wellington, where she became director of Va'aomanū Pasifika, home to Te Herenga Waka Victoria University's Pacific and Samoan studies programmes. A posthumous collection of her scholarship, poems and other writings, *Sweat and Salt Water*, compiled and edited by her sister Katerina Teaiwa and other editors, was published by Te Herenga Waka University Press and University of Hawai'i Press in 2021.

Tulia Thompson is of Fijian (Rukua village, Beqa), Tongan and Pākehā descent. She has a PhD in sociology and a Master's in creative writing from the University of Auckland. She writes poetry and essays. Her fantasy novel for 8- to 12-year-olds, *Josefa and the Vu*, was published by Huia in 2007.

Joshua Tau'aikata'ane Toumu'a is a young poet of Tongan, Papua New Guinean and Pākehā descent. In 2022 his poem 'Veitongo' won the National Schools Poetry Award from the International Institute of Modern Letters.

Rhegan Tu'akoi is a Tongan and Pākehā writer and poet. Her family hails from South Canterbury and the village of Holonga, Tongatapu. Her poetry has been published in *The Pantograph Punch*, *Sweet Mammalian*, *Mayhem Journal* and *Poetry New Zealand Yearbook*. She lives in Te Whanganui-a-Tara Wellington.

Tamara Tulitua (Sāfaʻatoʻa, Matāʻutu, Gagāifo, Vailima, Tanugāmanono, Sapapāliʻi) was the 2022 Emerging Pasifika Writer in Residence at the International Institute of Modern Letters, where she completed her Master's in creative writing in 2021.

Josua Tuwere has been writing poetry since attending high school at Suva Grammar in the 1980s, a period of great change in Fiji. His creative journey flourished at the University of the South Pacific in the 1990s as part of the Niu Waves Writers' Collective. He lives in Te Whanganui-a-Tara Wellington.

Losalini Tuwere says, 'I am from Fiji, specifically from Moala, Lau, with maternal links to Natewa, Cakaudrove. I am married with two children. Living away from Fiji for most of my adult life has limited my use of the Fijian language. Writing in Fijian is my way of capturing my oral language and passing it on.'

Tipesa Victoria Ulavale is from Sāmoa and is a student who lives in Te Whanganui-a-Tara Wellington.

Ailine Vakasiuola grew up in a Tongan household in the small town of Katikati surrounded by a strong Pasifika community. There are only three things she will read voluntarily: the Bible, poetry and anything about how Pasifika people are connected.

Māhina T. Valentine (Sāsina, Neiafu, Asau, Pākehā, Saleʻaula) is a poet, naturalist and artist living in Aotearoa. The Sāmoa Conservation Society received 333 per cent of her poem fee for the 'Save the Manumea' campaign. The critically endangered manumea is one of the closest living relatives of the iconic extinct dodo; its scientific name, *Didunculus strigirostris*, means 'little dodo'. Also known as the tooth-billed pigeon, the manumea is Sāmoa's beautiful, beloved national manu/bird. Faʻasao le manumea!

Kasi Valu says, 'Ko hoku hingoa ko Kasi Petelo Lennox Kelepi Valu. Oku lele mai mei Maʻufanga mo Lapaha. As an actor, poet, writer and producer for Le Moana under the leadership and vision of Tupe Lualua, my work centres on the experiences, wit, complexities and universality of our Pacific peoples.'

Jonah Vili is an East Auckland poet of Samoan descent and Bachelor of Arts graduate from the Manukau Institute of Technology. A proud father of two, he is writing poems in support of Aotearoa Lifeline and a children's book inspired by his grandson, Niko.

Jahra (Arieta) Wasasala is a Fijian-Pākehā poet, performer, choreographer and artist. Within the islands of Viti, Fiji, they hail from the provinces of Ba and Macuata. They live in Tāmaki Makaurau Auckland, drawing on visions as memory and the archive of embodiment.

Maualaivao Albert Wendt was born in Apia, Western Sāmoa, and lives in Tāmaki Makaurau Auckland. He is regarded internationally as one of the Pacific region's major novelists and poets. He has been publishing novels, short stories and poetry since the 1960s, and has won many honours and awards, including the Order of New Zealand. He holds the highest aliʻi title, Maualaivao, from the Aiga Sā-Maualaivao of Malie.

Gem Wilder (Fijian, Samoan, Irish, Scottish) is a Wellington-based writer. Their work has been published in a variety of places, including *The Spinoff*, *The Sapling*, *Sport*, *Is It Bedtime Yet?* and *Out Here*, and at Enjoy Gallery, The Dowse, Wellington Museum and LitCrawl.

Faith Wilson is a Samoan-Pālagi writer and publisher. She received a Master's in creative writing from the International Institute of Modern Letters in 2014, where she was awarded the Biggs Prize for Poetry. In 2021, she launched Saufoʻi Press, publishing poetry books by Moana Pacific writers in Aotearoa. She works as a project editor at Penguin Random House.

About the editors

David Eggleton is a poet and writer of Rotuman, Tongan and Pākehā heritage. His collection *The Conch Trumpet* (Otago University Press, 2015) won the 2016 Mary and Peter Biggs Award for Poetry at the 2016 Ockham New Zealand Book Awards. He also received the 2016 Prime Minister's Award for Literary Achievement in Poetry. David was the Aotearoa New Zealand Poet Laureate from 2019 to 2021.

Vaughan Rapatahana (Te Ātiawa, Ngāti Te Whiti) is a poet, novelist, writer and anthologist widely published across several genres in both his main languages, te reo Māori and English. He is a critic of the agencies of English language proliferation and the consequent decimation of Indigenous tongues. His most recent poetry collection, written in te reo Māori (with English language 'translations'), is titled *te pāhikahikatanga/ incommensurability*. It was published by Flying Islands Books in Australia in 2023.

Mere Taito is a poetry, flash fiction and short story writer and scholar of Rotuman heritage who is based in Kirikiriroa Hamilton. Her work has appeared in *Landfall, Bonsai,* and *Best New Zealand Poems* as well as in academic journals such as *International Education Journal.*

About the cover artist

Dagmar Vaikalafi Dyck is a New Zealand artist of Tongan and German descent. In 1995, she became the first woman of Tongan descent to graduate from Elam School of Fine Arts at the University of Auckland. She has been the recipient of numerous awards, scholarships and grants. Her artworks are held in both public and private collections in New Zealand and overseas.

Acknowledgements

We are grateful to artist Dagmar Vaikalafi Dyck for granting permission to reproduce her vibrant 2022 painting *a gift of thanks*, which is based on patterns and designs within early Tongan koloa, or decorated tapa, on the cover of this anthology.

We would also like to acknowledge the support and encouragement of Nicola Legat and her production team at Massey University Press for backing this project unhesitatingly and consistently. We thank Creative New Zealand, too, for an arts grant which has helped support this project.

We wish to thank the following people for their help in contacting some of the poets and/or supporting our youngest writers to complete their submission documents for this anthology: Fergus Barrowman (Te Herenga Waka University Press), Adrienne Jansen (Landing Press), David Douglas, Carol Rowse, Doug Poole (Blackmail Press), Sisilia Eteuati (Tatou Publishing), Dave Taylor (*Mayhem Journal*), Rebecca Hawkes and Nikki-Lee Birdsey (*Sweet Mammalian*), Nicola Manoa, Jordan Hamel (*Stasis*), Faith Wilson (*Tupuranga Journal*), Amiria Talo, Feana Tuʻakoi, Luisa Lolohea, Shelly Rao, Helen Tauʻau Filisi, Inangaro Vakaafi, Dr Jess Pasisi, Maureen Mariner Fepuleai, Andrea Low, Daren Kamali, Michael O'Leary and Josua Tuwere.

Index

First published in 2024 by Massey University Press
Private Bag 102904, North Shore Mail Centre
Auckland 0745, New Zealand
www.masseypress.ac.nz

Text copyright © individual contributors, 2024

Design by Megan van Staden
Cover artwork: Dagmar Vaikalafi Dyck, *a gift of thanks*, 2022

The moral rights of the authors and illustrators have been asserted

A catalogue record for this book is available from the National
Library of New Zealand

Printed and bound in China by Everbest Investment Ltd

ISBN: 978-1-99-101658-4

Thanks to all the publishers and copyright-holders who have given
permission to reproduce poems — a full list is provided in the
bibliography, see page 300.

The assistance of Creative New Zealand is gratefully acknowledged
by the publisher